ENCYCLOPEDIA
of
RIFLES & HANDGUNS

ENCYCLOPEDIA
of
RIFLES & HANDGUNS

A COMPREHENSIVE GUIDE TO FIREARMS

EDITED BY SEAN CONNOLLY

CHARTWELL
BOOKS, INC.

A QUINTET BOOK

Published by Chartwell Books
A Division of **BOOK SALES, INC.**
114 Northfield Avenue
Edison, New Jersey, 08837

This edition produced for sale in the U.S.A., its
territories and dependencies only.

ISBN 0-7858-0328-9

Reprinted 1995

This book was designed and produced by
Quintet Publishing Limited
6 Blundell Street
London N7 9BH

Creative Director: Richard Dewing
Designer: Neal Cobourne
Project Editor: Diana Steedman

The material in this publication previously appeared
in *Handguns* by Frederick Wilkinson; *Modern Handguns* by
Robert Adam; *The Guinness Encyclopedia of Weaponry* by
Ian V. Hogg; *The World's Most Powerful Rifles & Handguns*
by Robert Adam; *The New Illustrated Encyclopedia of Firearms*
by Ian V. Hogg.

Typeset in Great Britain by
Central Southern Typesetters, Eastbourne
Manufactured in Singapore by Eray Scan Pte Ltd.
Printed in Singapore by
Star Standard Industries (Pte) Ltd.

CONTENTS

INTRODUCTION

"So long as the infantry had a smooth-bore musket, and had thus no precision in action beyond 100 paces, it was little inclined to exact scientific researches. But the precision and the long range of the rifled weapon, and in particular the improvement of it due to various breech-loading systems, compelled the infantry to occupy themselves seriously with the trajectory, in order to see how far the precision and the range could be improved and the best possible infantry arm be obtained."

Letters on Artillery VII; Prince Kraft zu Hohenlohe-Ingelfingen, 1887.

IN MANY ways the arrival of gunpowder – with its power to propel projectiles – ushered in the modern era. The first European handguns helped cannons blow holes in Medieval notions of warfare.

Renaissance craftsmen refined these weapons, making them more portable and accurate, while gifted inventors such as Leonardo da Vinci laid the groundwork for quicker and safer means of igniting the charge. At the same time what had once been strictly military weaponry gradually became domestic. These early weapons, with their hand-tooled workings and intricate markings, were prized by their original owners – as they are now, in the hands of collectors.

The rifle reversed the trend by developing as a personal weapon and then proving itself in the field of battle. Imparting a spin to a discharged bullet increased its accuracy, and hunters were among the first to benefit from this advance. In the conflicts of the 18th and 19th centuries these new weapons could spell superiority in the "arms race". Many subsequent rifle developments were inspired or refined in combat.

This book traces the evolution of rifles and handguns, from the first clumsy weapons through all the major steps that led to their modern counterparts. It also examines the importance of ammunition and power – factors that continue to inspire developments more than six centuries after the first handguns appeared.

Along the way there are encounters with the ideas that led to new developments, and the people behind these ideas. The study of rifles and handguns acknowledges the brilliance of those who left their mark on gun-making – and on history itself. Many of these names have become emblematic of their age: von Dreyse, Forsyth, Ferguson, Colt, Remington, Smith and Wesson, Beretta, Luger and Mauser.

Some of the intensity of these innovators is reflected in the passions of those now involved with rifles and handguns. Collectors recognize the beauty and rarity not only of the guns themselves, but of the ammunition, gun-cases and advertisements relating to rifles and handguns. These passions spill over into the use of these weapons in target shooting contests and in the resurgence of hand-crafted weapons and ammunition. In a sense history has gone full-circle, with some modern producers attending to their weapons with a sense of wonder and pride that would not be out of place in a 17th-century workshop fashioning matchlock weapons.

THE FIRST SMALL ARMS

THE TERM "firearms" can be expanded to cover virtually anything that uses explosives to launch a projectile, but, for the purposes of this book we must be somewhat more precise, and adhere to the approved definitions of "small arms"—weapons that are less than 15.5 mm (0.60in) in caliber. The two figures are not identical, but simply represent the largest practical caliber for portable weapons in the metric and imperial systems of measurement. Beyond this, we are in the group of weapons usually defined as "automatic cannon"—weapons of 20mm and 30mm caliber—and beyond that we are into artillery—the "cannon" proper—where, if the late Dr. Gerald Bull, pioneer of the Iraqi "supergun" was to be believed, the sky is the limit.

The first definite reference to a firearm of any sort is in an English manuscript of 1326, "*De Officils Regnum*" ("On the Duties of Kings"), in which there is an illustration of a small cannon being fired, but it was not until the closing years of the century that technology had evolved sufficiently to allow the first "hand gonne" to appear. This was a development of the "ridaudequin," which appeared in about 1380; it consisted of a number of small-caliber cannon barrels mounted on a light cart, the barrels being splayed apart so as to deliver their shots in a fan-shaped arc to the front. While these weapons appear to have been effective, they had one major limitation. As they were fixed to their carts they could not deal with an enemy who suddenly appeared on the flanks. The logical step was to take on of the same barrels and attach it to a wooden pole, which could then be carried by one man. With the barrel loaded with powder and shot, and with the man holding a length of

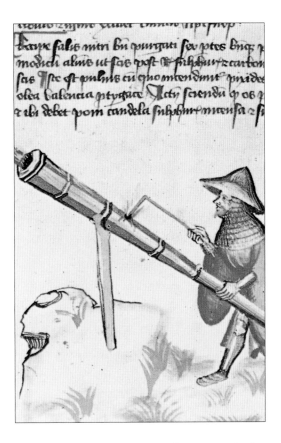

burning rope, he could tuck the pole under his arm should a target appear, roughly aiming the weapon, and touch it off by applying his burning "match" to the vent of the gun to ignite the gunpowder. In this manner, the portable handgun arrived on the battlefield.

The "hand gonne" was therefore the transitional stage between the cannon and the family of weapons that we collectively call "small arms." In the past, theories have been put forward that hand-held weapons must have preceded cannon, since it is customary to make things small at first and then enlarge them.

OPPOSITE
An early siege. Soldiers with handguns, accompanied by archers and artillery, lay siege to a castle in this illumination from a manuscript of Quinte Curce, completed in 1468.

LEFT
Illustration from a manuscript c.1400, showing a hand gonne being ignited.

BELOW
This bronze gun was found in Loshult, Sweden; it bears no marks, nor any indication of how it was mounted, but the reinforced muzzle suggests that it was an improved model based upon previous designs which had split at the muzzle, and therefore probably dates from the latter part of the 14th century.

However, in this case the custom was reversed, and for good reason: in experimenting with a substance as dangerous as gunpowder (see page 12) it was obviously better to make something heavy and strong and fire it at arm's length in order to gain some understanding of the effects before reducing it and bringing it closer to the human body.

The first handguns were simply reduced cannon, though because of their smaller size it was possible to cast them rather than build them up from strips of metal. The earliest known specimen is the "Tannenberg gun," so called from its discovery in a well at the ruins of the castle of Tannenberg (not the Tannenberg in former Prussia, but a small castle in Hesse). Since this castle was destroyed in 1399, the weapon must

ABOVE

This Japanese handgun is small enough to be used in one hand and appears to be ignited by a match. The muzzle, appearing from the mouth of a dragon, is a common Eastern decoration.

ABOVE

A cast barrel attached to the remains of its stock by an iron strap. This weapon is of interest since it shows a reduction in calibre from the original handguns, doubtless to make it more controllable in use. Tentatively dated as early 15th century it also shows the beginnings of ornamentation around the barrel and muzzle.

Handguns could be fired in various ways, depending upon how big they were and how experienced the use might be. Perhaps the safest method was to construct the stock so that it could be hooked over a wall or other support when fired. More often it was tucked beneath the arm and supported by one hand while he directed the match to the vent with the other. The need to watch the match and vent meant that aiming was tentative at best.

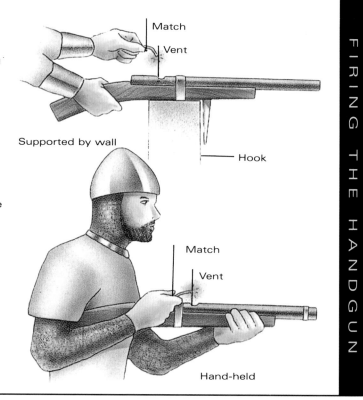

Match

Vent

Supported by wall

Hook

Match

Vent

Hand-held

FIRING THE HANDGUN

date from before that, and the existence of hand guns in the 14th century is borne out by the English Privy Wardrobe accounts for 1388 which record "III [3] cannons parvos vocatos handgunnes." The Tannenberg gun is cast of bronze, octagonal in section, weighing about 1.2kg (2½lb) And 32cm (12½in) long with an 18mm (¾in) bore. A bronze gun of similar date and hexagonal in shape was recovered from the sea off Morko in Sweden. Some guns were made of iron. One of the earliest known specimens was found at Vedelspang in Schleswig, Germany. This was another castle, which records show was destroyed in 1426.

ABOVE
A Bronze handgun with hook.

RIGHT
A mounted soldier with "petronel" and match.

RIGHT
Two Swiss handguns of the 14th century, one fitted with a recoil hook to become a "hakenbuchse."

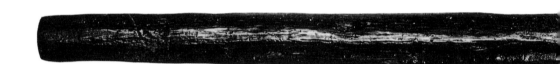

Gunpowder is an intimate mixture of saltpeter, charcoal, and sulfur: the earliest formula, that of Roger Bacon, gives the proportions as 7:5:5, or 41% saltpeter, 29.5% charcoal, and 29.5% sulfur. This gradually changed, the percentage of saltpeter increasing, until by the end of the 18th century it had reached its final form:

75% saltpeter, 15% charcoal, and 10% sulfur. The earliest powder was called "serpentine" and was a finely ground powder. This had certain defects: packed tightly in a gun chamber it was difficult to ignite and slow to burn, and in storage and transport had a distinct tendency to separate out its constituent parts. During the 15th century the

French invented "corned" powder, in which the three substances were mixed together in the wet state (which was a much safer method than dry mixing) and the resulting paste dried. This was then crumbled and passed through sieves to produce granular powder. Such powder was more efficient in the gun, since the interstices between

the grains allowed faster ignition and combustion, and since each grain was a solid compound the individual substances could not separate out. Early woodcuts show various stages in the making of powder: chopping the charcoal, wet-mixing the powder, breaking up the "press-cake" and sieving the grains.

GUNPOWDER

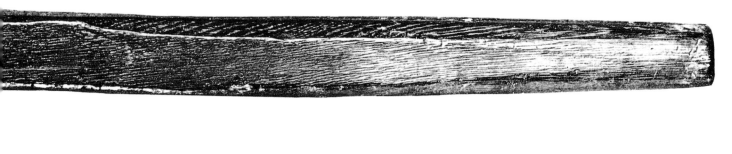

EARLY "HOOK GUNS"

Both the Morko gun and the Vedelspang gun have a large hook or lug beneath the barrel; in the former it is a forged lug with a loop shrunk onto the barrel, and in the latter it had been formed as part of the barrel. Its purpose was to anchor the gun against recoil by placing this hook over a wall or perhaps the side of a wagon, allowing the firer to direct the gun without danger from recoil when it was fired. The Morko gun, like most others had the barrel attached, usually by metal bands, to a long wooden stock which could be used to direct the gun. The Vedelspang gun had the barrel extended to form a long iron stock with a knob at the end, which was probably a convenient hand grip for the gunner.

Contemporary drawings show these "hook guns" in use in the early years of the 15th century. The drawings suggest that the use of the hook allowed the gunner to take a rudimentary aim by looking along the barrel. Yet already by 1411, some thought had been given to the mechanics of directing fire: a German engraving of that year shows a handgun with a "serpentine matchlock," an S-shaped piece of metal pivoted at its centre to the side of the stock. The forward end held a piece of burning slow-match, which, when the rear end was raised by the touch of a ginger, came into contact with the touch-hole. The gunner could use both hands to hold and fire, rather than trying to wedge it under his arm while at the same time having to manipulate a length of burning cord.

FROM HACKBUTT TO WHEEL-LOCK

BY THE early part of the 15th century the handgun began to change its form. The large-caliber weapons were difficult to fire while the serpentine matchlock made control slightly easier. Moreover the match had been moved to the side of the weapon, making it feasible to take some sort of aim across the top of the barrel. However, the long stock or tiller, tucked beneath the arm, made this impossible.

The handgun with the hook beneath the barrel, adapted for firing over walls or using some other solid rest to absorb recoil, now became the "hagbut" or "hackbut," a corruption of the German *hackenbusche*—"hook gun." In the past this has frequently been confused with the "arquebus", but the distinction between hackbut and arquebus (which often appears as harquebus) is apparent from a French document of 1527. It records the pay of "arquebusiers" and "hacbuttiers," noting that the latter were paid 10 times as much as the former, which suggests that the hackbut was somewhat more efficient than the arquebus. However, as the arquebus was improved it overtook the hackbut in general utility and by the latter half of the 16th century the hackbut was fast disappearing.

As the hackbut became lighter the need for the hook was reduced, since a man could support the recoil. The bore of the gun decreased, as did the size of the bullet and powder charge: the barrel was made lighter, longer, and more slender, giving better direction to the ball. All that remained was to make the gun controllable, and this was achieved by developing the first full stock, generally called the Lansknecht stock, after the German mercenaries who devised it. It consisted of a length of wood with a step in it so that the rear end of the barrel butted against the step while the whole barrel was supported by the wood and retained in place by iron straps. The rear end was shaped roughly to fit against the man's shoulder, and the usual type of serpentine lock was retained. Occasionally the wood was shaped to provide a better grip for the firer's hands.

Soon craftsmen began carving the butt and stock, decorating it, and, at the same time, developing the serpentine lock into a more compact and reliable form—the snapping matchlock. This improvement to the handgun led to

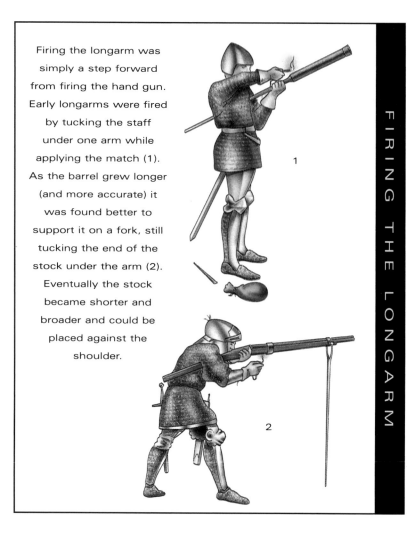

Firing the longarm was simply a step forward from firing the hand gun. Early longarms were fired by tucking the staff under one arm while applying the match (1). As the barrel grew longer (and more accurate) it was found better to support it on a fork, still tucking the end of the stock under the arm (2). Eventually the stock became shorter and broader and could be placed against the shoulder.

FIRING THE LONGARM

LEFT
From Jacques de Gheyn's **Manual of Arms** *(1607), the picture shows a typical arquebusier with his matchlock weapon and its firing rest. Note that he has the loose match gathered in his free hand, and that the match is lit at both ends; should the end in the cock be extinguished, it can be quickly relit from the free end.*

the arquebus, a long arm capable of being fired from the shoulder, though in practice it was common to use a forked rest to support the weight of the barrel.

With the weapon at his shoulder the soldier could now line up the barrel on his target with some degree of accuracy. To achieve greater accuracy rudimentary sights became more common. As early as 1450 there are examples of guns fitted with a simple blade foresight and an upright block with a notch for a rearsight. By 1500 a rearsight made by fixing two metal plates parallel to the barrel and filling the space between them with lead, then filing a groove in the lead, was in use. The earliest guns were so inaccurate that they could dispense with sights,

but as the accuracy improved, owing to better and more careful manufacture, the desire to hit the target led to gradual acceptance of sighting devices. By the middle of the 16th century competitive shooting, which would be virtually impossible without sights, was relatively common in Europe. Not only were there contests between firearms, but contemporary engravings show that contests between firearms and crossbows were frequently held, and honors were evenly divided.

MATCHLOCK AND WHEEL-LOCK

The first attempt at mechanically firing a handgun was the serpentine, a curved piece of metal with a lighted match at one end that could be

ABOVE
An engraving by Theodore de Bry, dated 1594, showing Spanish Conquistadors herding prisoners. The matchlock is well in evidence, with typically Spanish curved stocks and simple handgrip triggers. The men with firearms have retained their swords for close-quarter fighting.

brought into contact with the touch-hole of the cannon. To make this idea effective it was necessary to enlarge the mouth of the touch-hole into a pan, in which powder could be sprinkled, thus giving a larger ignition area and decreasing the need for an accurate and therefore difficult connection with the match.

The next step was to make the serpentine less cumbersome, and thus the "snapping matchlock" evolved. In this system, which appeared in about 1500, the burning match was held at the tip of a curved arm which was hinged to the stock of the weapon. A short lever bore against this arm, keeping it away from the touch-hole, and a rod, through the stock, was attached to this lever so that pressure on the rod by the firers thumb or finger would disengage the lever and allow the curved arm to fall by its own weight and so bring the match into contact with the powder.

The match referred to was a length of tow, twisted from hemp, flax, or cotton and then soaked in a strong solution of saltpeter and allowed to dry. When ignited it burned at about one inch per minute, and a suitable length could be clamped into the end of the curved arm and ignited before battle commenced. An even slower rate of burning could be achieved by varying the stretch of the saltpeter solution.

The snapping matchlock was only in used for a relatively brief period during the 16th century, although a number of them eventually found

A B O V E

A German soldier of the early 17th century armed with a matchlock musket. He carries a powder flask over his shoulder and is busy ramming the ball on top of the powder charge.

After removing the rammer he will pull the match back to a safe position and then charge the pain with powder. Note that he also carries a sword.

B E L O W

A richly decorated Italian 17th-century matchlock gun, with the match cord carried in its holder. The lever-shaped trigger brought the burning match into contact with the priming powder in the pan. The stock is inlaid with pierced brass work and the barrel decorated with silver.

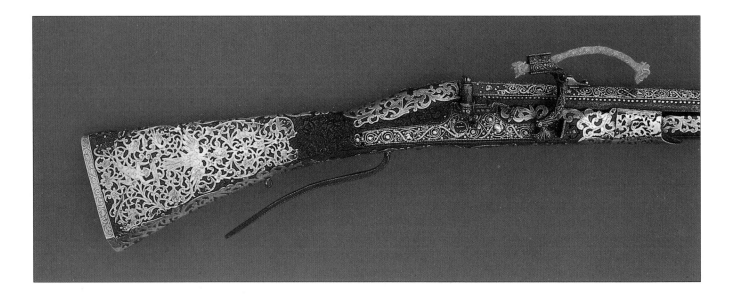

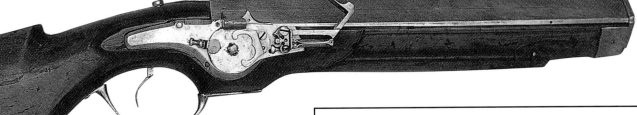

A B O V E

A German wheel-lock carbine dating from about 1620. The squared end of the wheel axle, upon which the spanner fits, can be seen, the wheel being concealed within the lock casing. The cock, holding the pyrites, is folded forward in the "safe" position and the pan cover is closed.

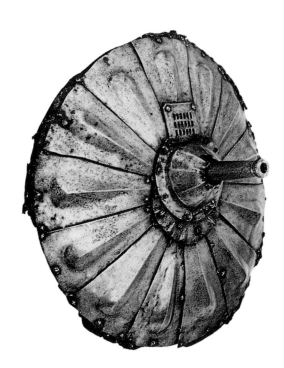

A B O V E

A breech-loading matchlock shield-pistol belonging to Henry VIII.

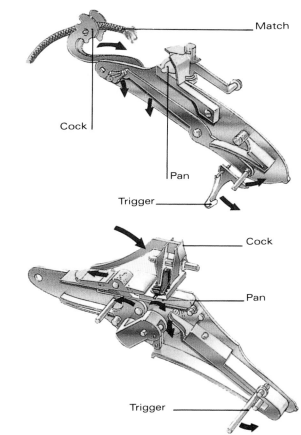

Match

Cock

Pan

Trigger

Cock

Pan

Trigger

Operating the matchlock

Once loaded, the cock was pulled back and the pan filled with powder, the match was then clamped into the jaws of the cock. Pressing the trigger then released the cock to fly forward and bring the match into contact with the powder, so igniting the charge.

Operating the wheel-lock

The cock was pulled to full cock position, the pan loaded with powder and the cover closed. The striking wheel was then wound up. On pulling the trigger the pan cover slid away, the wheel spun, the cock fell and brought the pyrites into contact with the serrated edge, and sparks ignited the charge.

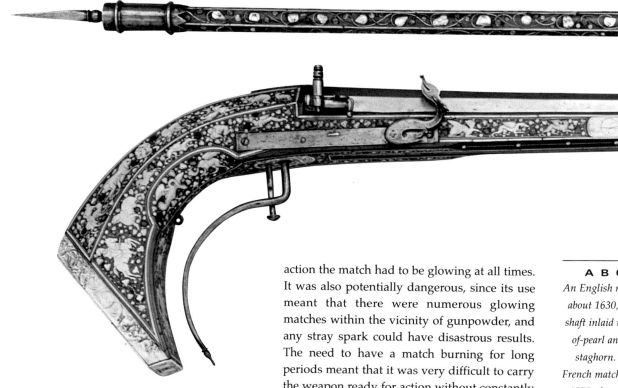

their way to Japan and the system was adopted there and remained in use until the middle of the 19th century. In Europe the snapping matchlock was replaced first by a primitive trigger mechanism, derived from that used on the crossbow, and then by a neater trigger and sear mechanism concealed within a lock mechanism inserted into the stock. The curved arm was given a notch into which a metal strut fitted, and a spring to propel it forward. The strut was controlled by the trigger, so that pressure on the trigger removed the strut and allow the match arm to be driven forward by the spring to make contact with the powder in the touch-hole. In this form the matchlock survived as a military system until the latter part of the 18th century, largely because of its cheapness and simplicity.

The wheel-lock This matchlock musket was heavy and cumbersome, and its use was somewhat limited in that to be ready for instant action the match had to be glowing at all times. It was also potentially dangerous, since its use meant that there were numerous glowing matches within the vicinity of gunpowder, and any stray spark could have disastrous results. The need to have a match burning for long periods meant that it was very difficult to carry the weapon ready for action without constantly replacing the match as it burnt away. There was certainly no way in which a matchlock weapon, primed and ready for use, could be carried in a pocket or holster.

By 1530—from the evidence of a dated pistol in the Royal Armory of Madrid—the wheel-lock had been invented, introducing the first self-contained ignition system. Although it appears to have originated in Italy, the wheel-lock seems to have attained its greatest perfection in Germany, and many elegant German specimens have survived.

The wheel, from which the lock derives its name, has a serrated edge and revolves immediately behind, and partially into, the powder pan leading to the touch-hole and barrel. A short chain is attached to the axle of the wheel and to a powerful leaf spring; the axle has an exposed square end to enable a spanner to turn the wheel backward against the pressure of the spring. When the wheel is turned back sufficiently far, a peg enters a hole or recess in the wheel and is retained there by the trigger mechanism. A "dog" or "cock"—a hinged arm—carries a piece of iron pyrites clamped in its jaw and is also under spring pressure and re-

ABOVE
An English musket rest of about 1630, the wooden shaft inlaid with mother-of-pearl and engraved staghorn. Below it a French matchlock of about 1575, the walnut stock inlaid with engraved and stained staghorn.

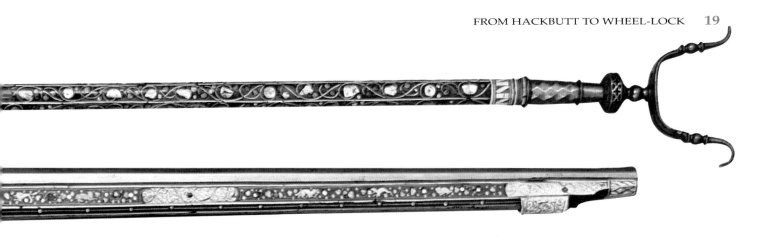

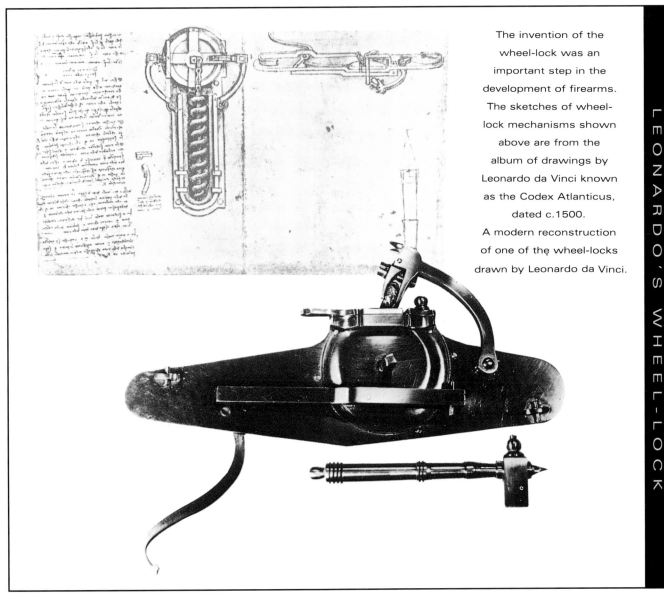

The invention of the wheel-lock was an important step in the development of firearms. The sketches of wheel-lock mechanisms shown above are from the album of drawings by Leonardo da Vinci known as the Codex Atlanticus, dated c.1500. A modern reconstruction of one of the wheel-locks drawn by Leonardo da Vinci.

LEONARDO'S WHEEL-LOCK

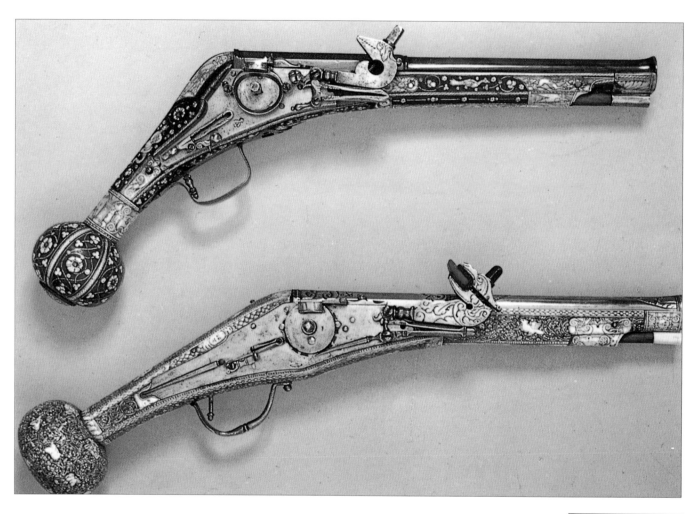

tained by a catch linked to the trigger. Pressing the trigger then releases the dog which swings over and strikes the circumference of the wheel, which has also been released and is spinning forward. The serrated edge strikes sparks from the pyrites, and the sparks fall into the pan and fire the weapon.

A variety of methods to achieve this mechanical end were developed over the two centuries during which the wheel-lock prospered. A pan cover was soon adopted, keeping the powder dry and in place, linked to either the wheel or cock so that it opened automatically as the sparks were struck. Some mechanisms used gearing to make spinning the wheel easier, or to make it rotate longer, while others used the movement of pulling the cock forward— "cocking" the weapon—to wind up the wheel spring and thus perform both actions at once. Less common were locks that used merely a

segment of the wheel (the "sector lock") or even a flat piece of metal with teeth (the "rasp lock").

The development of the wheel-lock was a major step in the evolution of firearms, since it meant that a weapon could be carried cocked— ready to fire—at any time, without the need for a cumbersome burning match. The weapon could thus be drawn and fired with one hand, making possible a one-handed weapon, the pistol. This concept was weclomed by the cavalry, who were now able to carry a firearm into action. It was soon appreciated that these new weapons constituted a serious security problem, since an assassin could conceal a weapon until he was close to his unsuspecting target. As early as 1517 Emperor Maximilian I of Austria (1459–1519) enacted restrictive laws against the carrying of self-ignited handguns—an early example of legal restrictions on firearms, a process that continues today.

THE SIMPLER FLINTLOCK

PEOPLE HAD used flint to strike sparks for many thousands of years, so it was not surprising that this system should be applied to firearms; the only problem lay in how to achieve it. The flintlock appeared in the 16th century, though the exact origin of its birthplace is in some doubt.

Very likely, the first was the Spanish lock or "miquelet," of which there is record as early as 1547. It was probably developed by Simon Marquette, the son of an Italian gunmaker who had settled in Spain. It consisted of a cock with jaws, which gripped a piece of flint, and a frizzen, an angled steel plate which covered the priming pan and also intercepted the fall of the spring-driven cock when the trigger was pulled. After the weapon was loaded with powder and ball, the cock was pulled back until a cross-bolt, or sear, moved across the lock frame to hold it back. The frizzen was then hinged forward to expose the pan, powder sprinkled into the pan,

A B O V E

A pair of snaphaunce pistols with mounts of chiselled iron by Giuseppe Guardiani of Anghiari. Italian, late 18th century.

B O T T O M

A German snaphaunce lock, inner and outer views.

R I G H T

A 17th century Russian snaphaunce, decorated in gilt.

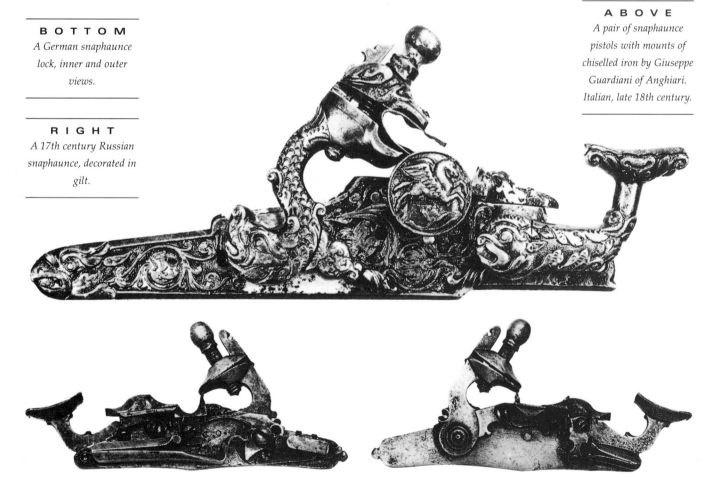

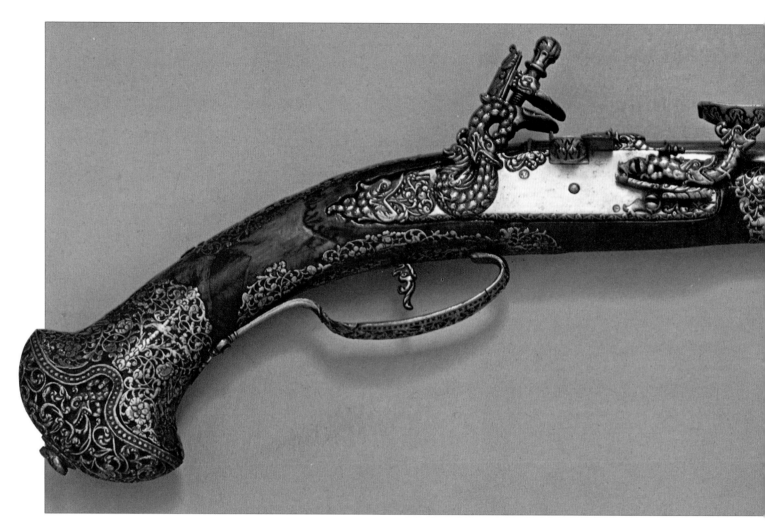

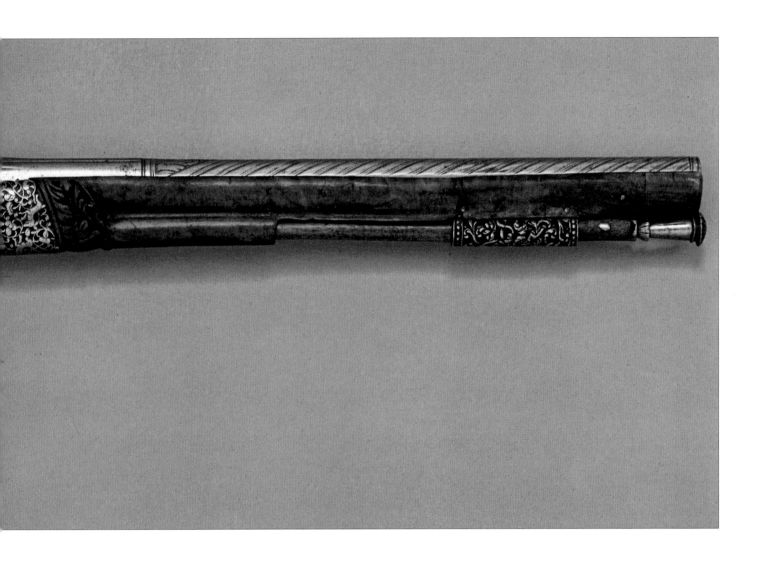

and the frizzen pulled back to cover the an and hold the powder in place. On pulling the trigger forward, and the flint struck the flat rear face of the frizzen. This struck sparks from the flint, and the impact also knocked the frizzen forward, exposing the powder in the pan to the falling sparks.

At much the same time as the "miquelet" the Dutch "snaphaunce" lock appeared. This used the same elements as the Spanish lock but was different in some important respects. The mainspring pulled the cock rather than pushing it, and the frizzen acted only to strike sparks. The pan cover was a separate, sliding component with a rod to link it to the cock, so that as the cock moved forward it pushed the pan cover open. Another significant difference was that the Spanish lock carried its spring on the outside, where it could be easily repaired, whereas the Dutch lock carried it inside, where it was better protected against damage.

Once these two locks had been introduced, variations followed. The English "dog-lock" appears to have been derived from the Dutch lock and takes its name from the addition of a "dog," or small hook, on the side of the lock frame behind the cock. On pulling back the cock, this hook snapped into a recess in the cock to hold it at the "half cock" position from which it could not be fired by using the trigger. The only way to fire was to pull back the cock to the full-cock position, then thumb the dog out of the way while pulling the trigger. In addition, the English adopted the Spanish system of making

DIRECT

A snaphaunce holster-pistol, the walnut stock inlaid with mounts of pierced iron, the barrels signed "Lazarino Cominazzo"; Brescia, about 1650.

the frizzen and pan cover in one piece but kept the Dutch method of concealing the mainspring inside the lock.

The Swedish lock used a long and slender cock which appears to have been influenced by the matchlock, giving this lock a distinctive appearance. The separate frizzen and concealed spring of the Dutch lock was used, but the pan cover was not connected to the cock and had to be opened before pulling the trigger.

THE FRENCH FLINTLOCK

After studying these variations, the French perfected the mechanism into the final flintlock design, the French lock. Their first attempt resembled the Dutch design, but without the interconnected pan cover. Their principal innovation was the "tumbler," a shaped cam inside the lock on the rotating shaft which carried the cock. The tumbler had notches which engaged with the trigger to give full- and half-cock positions and also a notch for the mainspring to provide the driving force for the cock.

This was soon superseded by the perfected French model which eventually became the

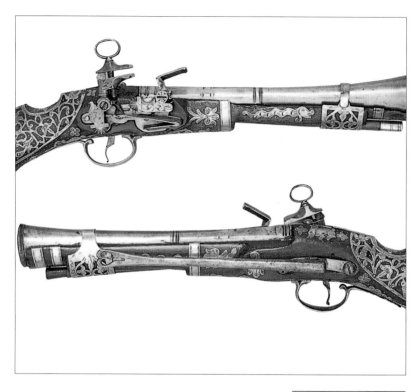

A B O V E
*Two Spanish miquelet-lock blunderbusses,
c.1690.*

A B O V E
Brown Bess was the flintlock musket that armed British soldiers for 200 years. Here, the lock is in the fired position; the cock has gone forward and knocked the frizzen so as to strike sparks and reveal the pan with the priming powder. Note the maker's name, "Grice 1759," and the Royal monogram indicating a military weapon.

The powder and shot could be loaded before or after priming the pan.

The usual military practice was to prime the pan before loading the barrel. To prime, the cock was drawn back, usually to the half-cock position, the frizzen opened (top), and fine powder sprinkled into the pan from a powder flask. The frizzen was then snapped shut and the cock drawn back to the full-cock position.

On the order "Present!" the weapon was raised and pointed at the target; on "Fire!" the trigger was pulled, releasing the cock to fly forward and strike the frizzen. This generated sparks, and the blow of the cock threw the frizzen forward, exposing the powder in the pan to the falling sparks, so igniting the charge in the barrel.

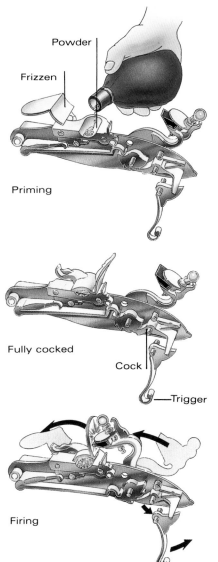

Powder

Frizzen

Priming

Fully cocked

Cock

Trigger

Firing

OPERATING THE FLINTLOCK

accepted standard. For this the French went back to the Spanish lock and the one-piece frizzen and pan cover, shaping it more carefully to ensure certain ignition and opening. Together with the tumbler, the new frizzen made the French lock as foolproof and reliable as possible, and from its appearance in about 1635 to the end of the flintlock era some 200 years later there was very little improvement in the design. The flintlock had several advantages over the older, wheel-lock; first, its reliability of action; its ease of maintenance, especially since flint was more readily obtainable and much more durable than the pyrites demanded by the wheel system; and third, its cheapness, since it was much simpler and easier to make than the complicated wheel-lock. Adoption of the flintlock was a cheap method of equipping whole armies with reliable firearms using mechanical ignition. While a master gunsmith could make a flintlock that was a thing of beauty and grace, a blacksmith could make a less graceful but just as effective and reliable one. The development of the flintlock was instrumental in lowering the price of firearms and spreading their ownership and use.

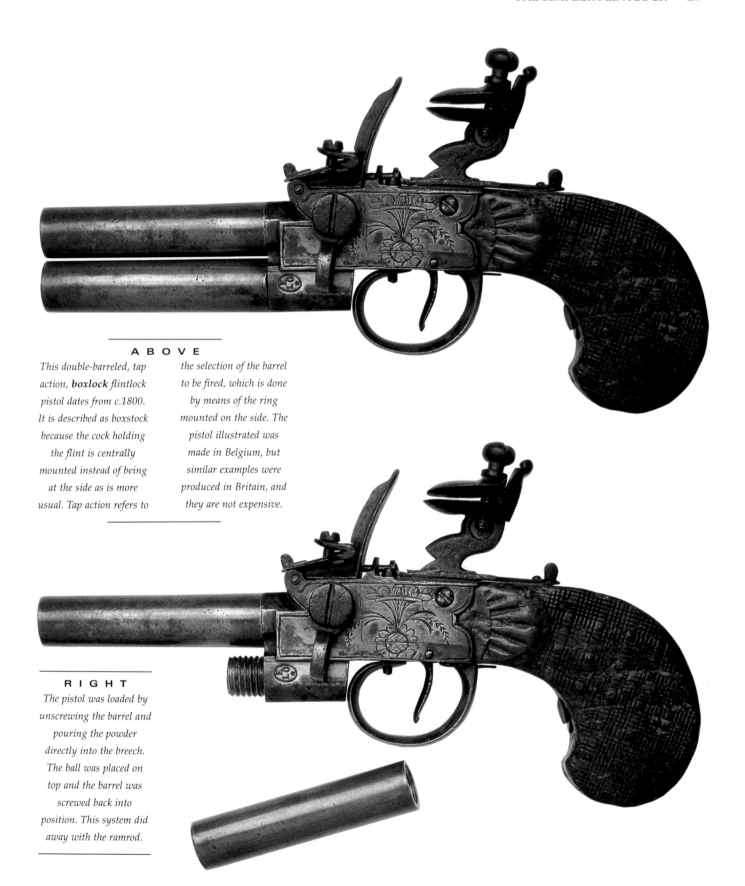

ABOVE

This double-barreled, tap action, **boxlock** flintlock pistol dates from c.1800. It is described as boxstock because the cock holding the flint is centrally mounted instead of being at the side as is more usual. Tap action refers to the selection of the barrel to be fired, which is done by means of the ring mounted on the side. The pistol illustrated was made in Belgium, but similar examples were produced in Britain, and they are not expensive.

RIGHT

The pistol was loaded by unscrewing the barrel and pouring the powder directly into the breech. The ball was placed on top and the barrel was screwed back into position. This system did away with the ramrod.

BIRTH OF THE RIFLE

A GUN'S ACCURACY is improved by rifling, that is the cutting of helical grooves inside the barrel. If the projectile can be made to expand into or otherwise grip these grooves, it will spin on its longer axis as it moves up the barrel. This will stabilize the projectile, ensuring that it remains nose-first during flight. The ball fired from a smooth bore barrel has no such stability. It will fly off in the direction opposite the last contact it makes with the barrel's interior, leading to inaccurate shooting.

Rifling first appeared towards the end of the 14th century. Gunmakers in Nuremberg are given the credit for its invention. For a long time its value was not appreciated. The lead ball of the day had to be driven down with a ramrod and mallet to engrave it into the rifling as it was loaded, and this frequently deformed it so much that it was no longer round and it few erratically. The poor-quality gunpowder, which left hard fouling encrusted in the barrel, was another drawback to rifling. Indeed, some guns had straight grooves, largely to allow the fouling to collect in them and thus leave what was virtually a smoothbore, though clean, barrel.

At first rifles were precision weapons for sporting use, where time spent reloading was not vital. It was some two centuries before rifling was taken up by the military, and even then rifles were used only by specialist troops. Christian IV of Denmark had wheel-lock rifles made for some of his troops in about 1600 and some French cavalry were issued with rifles by 1680.

The American Revolution (1775–1783) led to the more general acceptance of the rifle as a military weapon. The American frontiersmen

A B O V E

Lieutenant Colonel Patrick Ferguson began designing his rifle in 1774. He demonstrated it before the king at Windsor and before officers at Woolwich, resulting in orders for 100 rifles. Ferguson supervised manufacture, trained a company of men in the use of the rifle, and sailed for America in 1777.

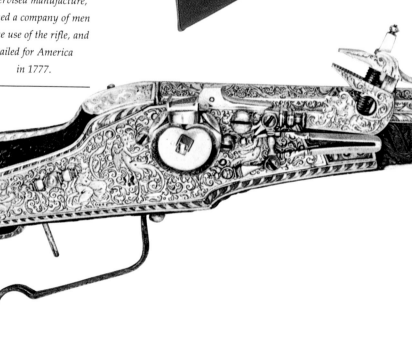

with their hunting rifles showed that they could outshoot the British soldiers with their smoothbore muskets, and so the British too adopted the rifles. The most notable weapon was the Ferguson, a breech-loading rifle that used a vertical screw to close the breech. Loading from the breech avoided all the problems of muzzle loading and in this regard the well-made Ferguson rifle was ahead of its time. Colonel Patrick Ferguson, the inventor, took a company armed with his rifle to America, where the rifle performed well. But when Colonel Ferguson was killed (ironically, by an American rifleman) in 1780 his company was disbanded.

Although these weapons demonstrated the accuracy and ranging power of rifled arms, it was the rifle's slow rate of fire, due to the time it took to load, which argued against its widespread military adoption. The rifleman had to load his powder; then place a greased patch accurately over the muzzle; place the ball upon it, ram it gently so as not to distort the ball, and get it into the exact position relative to the

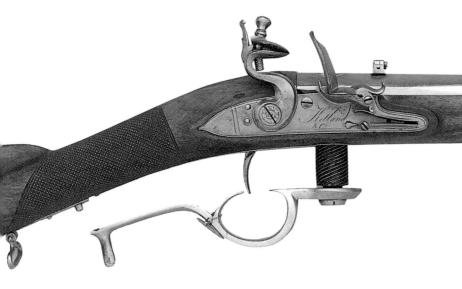

charge. Britain's Rifle Corps, issued with the Baker rifle in 1800, considered one shot a minute to be an acceptable rate of fire.

The difficulty in loading muzzle-loaders was eventually overcome by Captain Gustave Delvigne of France, who devised a rifle with a chamber of smaller diameter. Once the powder was loaded, the ball (which was an easy fit in the bore) came to rest against the end of the chamber and was then expanded into the rifling by a few taps with the ramrod. A rifle of this design was adopted by the French in 1842. Delvigne continued with his experiments and discovered that the best shape for a bullet was a cylinder with a conical nose. However, it took several years before he could convince the French army to adopt his alternative to the ball.

The next advance was the pillar breech of Colonel Thouvenin, in which the chamber had a central pillar and the powder was loaded around it. The conical bullet dropped down the bore to rest on the pillar and, again, a tap or two with the ramrod caused the end of the bullet to be expanded into the grooves.

THE SELF-EXPANDING BULLET

The final step was the Minié bullet, which was self-expanding. At its base it carried a thin iron cup, which when struck by the gases from the explosion of the cartridge, forced the skirt of the bullet outwards into the rifling. By the time this was perfected in the 1850s, the French Army had decided to adopt a breech-loader. However, the Minié bullet was used extensively during the Civil War (1861–1865) where it was the most common round used by both the Confederate and the Union armies.

The amount of twist in the rifling is critical to achieving the required degree of stability for the bullet. By making the rifling only just stabilize the bullet, its power to cause physical injury is increased because of its rapid destabilization on impact. On the other hand, a twist of rifling that overspins the bullet will increase its penetrative power, but reduce its capacity to wound. The size of a bullet is also important. Projectiles that are more than about eight times as long as their caliber (diameter) cannot be successfully spin-stabilized.

To put less stress on the projectile, progressive

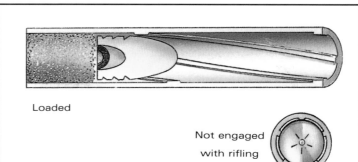

Loaded

Not engaged
with rifling

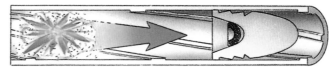

Firing

Engaged
with rifling

The essential feature of the Minié bullet was its expansion. The bullet did not catch in the rifling as it was rammed down the bore during loading. When the charge exploded, the gas

pressure acted on the cup in the base and forced the thinner skirt outwards to engage with the rifling, so generating spin as the billet was driven up the bore.

MINIÉ BULLET

or increasing twist rifling is often used. This starts with straight grooves, or a very slow twist, so that as the projectile accelerates up the bore it takes up spin gradually. The degree of twist then increases along the bore to the optimum, which continues to the muzzle. Progressive rifling is common in artillery, which uses heavy projectiles. Under high acceleration a heavy projectile could easily shear its connection with the rifling if the speed of its rotation were increased too rapidly.

In recent years high-velocity artillery has reverted to smooth-bore barrels, using fins to stabilize projectiles, in an attempt to obtain the highest possible velocities for the penetration of armour. A rifled gun wastes a proportion of the propelling energy in overcoming the friction of the rifling; the absence of this drag allows higher velocities to be achieved.

THE PERCUSSION SYSTEM

THE SEQUENCE of events in firing a flintlock weapon—the strike of sparks from the flint, the ignition of the powder in the pan, and finally the explosion of the propelling charge in the gun chamber—takes time. This did not matter so much to the military, but in game shooting it often led to the intended prey being frightened away before the ball could reach it. The flint system was also easily affected by rain—which was a more serious drawback for the military. Ingenious inventors of the time looked for ways to overcome these problems.

A first step was Edward C. Howard's discovery, in 1799, of "fulminating" materials—which would explode or ignite when struck. However, because of their extreme sensitivity to handling it was some time before any practical application was found. Eventually, the Reverend Alexander Forsyth, vicar of Belhevie in Scotland and a keen game shooter, discovered a method—the percussion lock—which he patented in 1807. This employed the mechanism of a flintlock, except that the cock did not carry a flint, but a suitably shaped hammerhead. In place of the

pan and frizzen, a hollow bolt led into the gun's chamber, and revolving on the outer end of this bolt was a tubular magazine. The gun was loaded with powder and ball in the normal way, and the magazine was filled with Forsyth's "fulminating mixture," a combination of mercury fulminate and potassium chlorate. The magazine was then twisted through a half-circle to deposit a small quantity of mixture in the tube leading to the chamber. Twisting the magazine back moved the mixture-carrying part out of the way so that a solid section, carrying a short movable rod, sat above the vent and the priming charge. Squeezing the trigger made the hammer fall and strike the rod, which drove down and struck the priming composition. This fired, igniting in turn the powder in the chamber.

Forsyth offered his invention to the Master-General of the Ordnance in London, who was responsible for the weapons used by the British Army. But before he could perfect his design the whole scheme was abandoned because of the prejudices of army traditionalists. Forsyth,

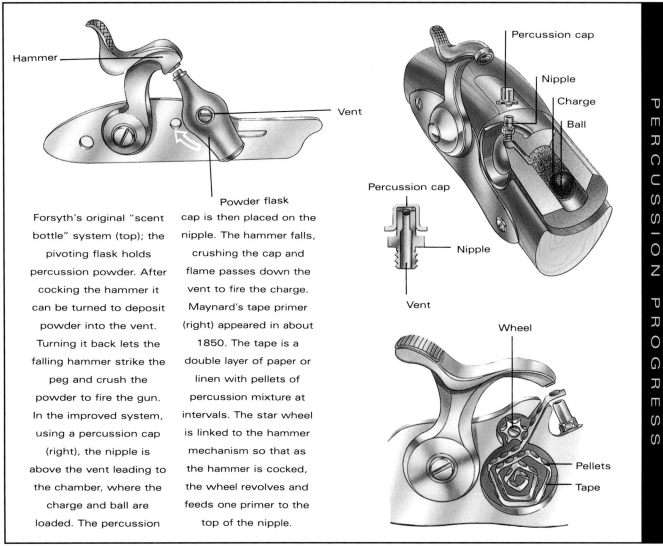

Forsyth's original "scent bottle" system (top); the pivoting flask holds percussion powder. After cocking the hammer it can be turned to deposit powder into the vent. Turning it back lets the falling hammer strike the peg and crush the powder to fire the gun. In the improved system, using a percussion cap (right), the nipple is above the vent leading to the chamber, where the charge and ball are loaded. The percussion cap is then placed on the nipple. The hammer falls, crushing the cap and flame passes down the vent to fire the charge. Maynard's tape primer (right) appeared in about 1850. The tape is a double layer of paper or linen with pellets of percussion mixture at intervals. The star wheel is linked to the hammer mechanism so that as the hammer is cocked, the wheel revolves and feeds one primer to the top of the nipple.

PERCUSSION PROGRESS

however, promoted his idea commercially with considerable success before his death in 1843.

THE PERCUSSION CAP

In 1818, once the percussion idea was shown to work, improvement soon followed. Joe Manton, the famous English gunsmith, invented a percussion tube, a thin copper tube that was inserted into the vent of the gun and struck by the falling hammer. However, removing the spent tube could prove difficult. A better idea was the percussion cap, which had first appeared in about 1814. This resembled a small metal top hat in section, with a layer of fulminating mixture in the "crown." The gun was made with a tubular extension from the vent—called the nipple—which was shaped so that the cap could be pressed over the open end to fit snugly. When the hammer fell onto the cap, it crushed the mixture between the cap and the mouth of the tube, and the flash of the exploding mixture went through the tube and into the gun chamber to light the gunpowder. The hammer usually had a recessed head which enclosed the cap at the moment of firing, so as to prevent fragments of copper, split off by the explosion, from injuring the shooter. After firing, the shooter cocked the hammer and removed the remains of the cap from the nipple.

Although the metal percussion cap was eventually adopted almost universally, other percussion systems were tried. One was the pill

lock, patented by Manton in 1816. This was an open pan that used fulmination composition pressed into small pills or tablets. When a pill was placed in the pan, the falling hammer crushed it, sending the flash into the gun. Another idea was percussion caps made from oiled paper which could be placed against a suitable vent and struck by the hammer (a system still used in children's cap pistols). In the tape primer—invented by Edward Maynard of the United States – a double paper tape containing pellets of fulmination composition was carried in a magazine in the lock. The action of cocking the hammer each time advanced a fresh length of tape and pellets. Large numbers of Maynard tape-primed rifles were used in the Civil War.

SAMUEL COLT AND THE REVOLVER

THE INVENTION of the percussion cap opened up new horizons for gunmakers, but the biggest changes probably occurred in the design of multishot weapons. The flintlock had been just a little too awkward to adapt to weapons firing more than three or four shots. Some flintlock revolvers had been made, but these were expensive to produce, rather cumbersome, and not too reliable.

The man responsible for the biggest advances came from Connecticut. His name has become almost synonymous with the revolver—Samuel Colt (1814–1862). Although he did not invent the revolver, for it had been known since the 16th century, Colt revolutionized the design and, even more importantly, introduced a system of mass production for such weapons. He produced a revolver with a cylinder that was drilled with five or six chambers, each with

its own short tube or nipple to hold a percussion cap. Pulling back the hammer activated a simple linkage system, which rotated the cylinder and brought a loaded chamber into line with the barrel. Pressing the trigger allowed the hammer to fall forwards and strike the uppermost cap and so fire the first shot. The process could be repeated until all the shots were discharged.

Colt's first venture into the arms business was not a great success, but by luck and perseverance he remained in business, and in 1848 he produced the heavy Dragoon revolver, which fired six shots of .44in caliber. He continued to manufacture this weapon with minor constructional differences over the next few years, ceasing production in 1861. In 1848 he also began supplying a smaller version, the Pocket Colt, which fired a .31in diameter bullet.

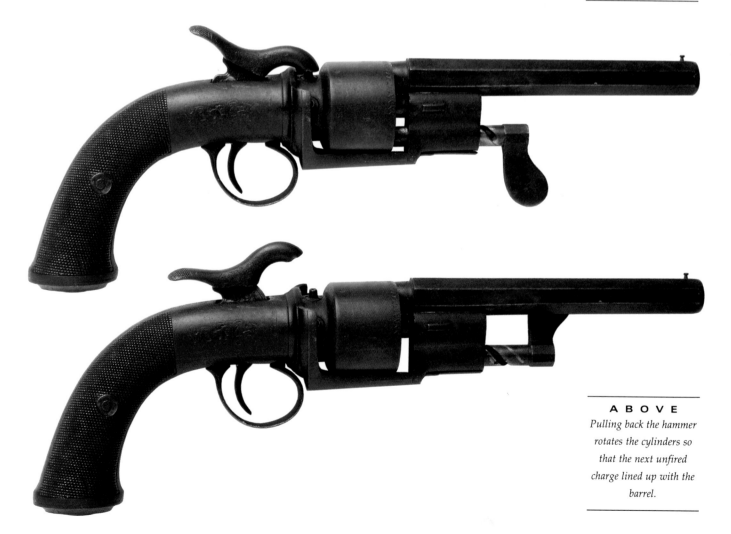

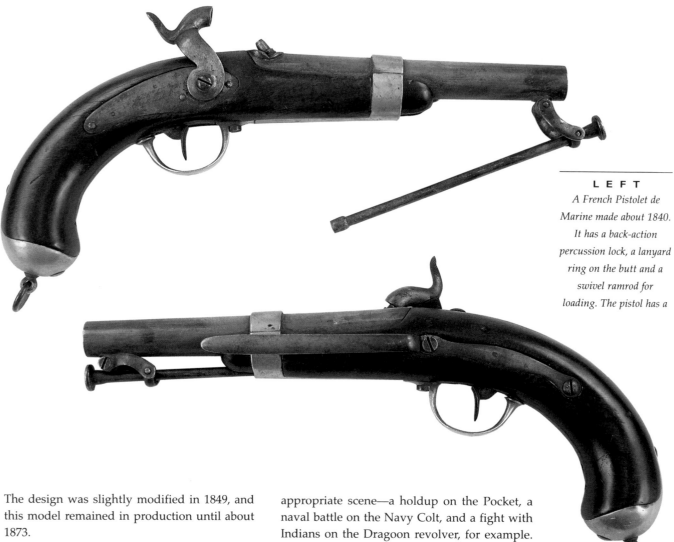

The design was slightly modified in 1849, and this model remained in production until about 1873.

In 1851 he introduced the larger Belt pistol, which is more commonly known as the Navy Colt, with a caliber of .36in, and this was also kept in production until about 1873. It was an accurate and reliable pistol, and about 40,000 were produced.

In 1851 the Great Exhibition of Trade and Industry was held in London's Hyde Park, and Colt decided to attend and display his products. By dint of presenting examples of his revolver to well-known public figures and through publicity and general showmanship he made a great impact on the British market, to the annoyance of the British gunmakers. They were even more upset when he set up a factory in Pimlico, London, to manufacture his revolvers.

All of these early Colt revolvers conform to a general style, with a cylinder engraved with an appropriate scene—a holdup on the Pocket, a naval battle on the Navy Colt, and a fight with Indians on the Dragoon revolver, for example. The barrels, which were produced in a variety of lengths, were stamped with varying legends, including an address. These markings make it possible to distinguish those produced in the London factory from the American-produced weapons, although some interchanging of parts did take place.

In 1856 Colt started production of his New Model Pocket revolver, which featured a side-mounted hammer for easy maintenance, but in 1861 he reverted to the old style with a Pocket Model but of the Navy caliber, .36in. In 1860 he made a larger, .44in caliber revolver, known as the New Model Army or Holster pistol, and this featured a round barrel with a loading lever that was used to press down the bullet into the chamber, which was streamlined into the barrel housing. He used a similar styling for his new

RIGHT
A Dragoon 3rd Model
Percussion Revolver with
Holster c1853/4. This
weapon belonged to
Captain Francis T. Bryan
of the US Army and saw
service on the American
frontier. A heavy weapon,
it fired a bullet of .44in
caliber. The cylinder was
engraved with a scene of a
fight with plains Indians.
All of Colt's early
revolvers were single
action, which means that
the hammer had to be
pulled back before the
trigger could be pressed to
fire the weapons.

ABOVE
Produced from 1871 until
1876, the Colt House
pistol preceded the Single
Action Army Revolver in
developing metallic
cartridge revolvers.
Because of the shape of
the cylinder, the four-shot
version was known as the
Cloverleaf model. Several
versions were made in
.41in long or short
rimfire, and some were
issued with ordinary
round cylinders.

RIGHT

RIGHT

A percussion revolver produced by William Tranter, a well-known British gunmaker. This 120-bore example has a double-trigger action. The longer section rotates the cylinder and cocks the action, while the portion inside the trigger guard actually fires the shot. The side-mounted ramrod was used during loading to force the bullet down into the chamber.

LEFT

A 38-bore Adams percussion revolver, dating from the mid-19th century. It is a self-cocking weapon because there is no easy means of pulling back the hammer apart from squeezing the trigger. Well made and sturdy, this was a direct competitor with the Colt, and there was much contemporary debate on the relative virtues of the two manufacturers.

Navy revolver in .36in caliber as well as on the Police Model.

Colt's London factory did not survive long but, stimulated by his example, many British manufacturers began to explore the revolver market. One of the leading makers was Robert Adams, who was soon in production with a large-caliber percussion revolver. The design of the Adams revolver differed from those made by Colt in many respects, but one major difference was in the method of firing. Colt's revolvers were all single action, which means that to fire a shot the hammer had to be pulled back manually, usually with the thumb. At the first click—the half cock—the cylinder could be rotated freely for loading, and, when ready, the hammer was pulled further back and locked in this position, which is known as cocked. The trigger was then pressed and the hammer, driven by a spring housed in the butt, swung forward to fire the shot. Adams's early revolvers had no spur on the hammer, which could be cocked manually only with great difficulty. Pressure on the trigger rotated the cylinder, cocked the hammer and, as pressure was maintained, allowed it to fall forward, to fire the weapon.

There was much debate as to which was the better system, and cogent arguments were provided on both sides. It was claimed that single action made for more careful shooting, while Adams's system enabled more rapid fire but required greater pressure on the trigger, which made aiming more difficult because the revolver tended to turn slightly in the hand. Using a mechanical system patented by Lieutenant Frederick Beaumont, Adams produced a double action weapon, which could be fired using either method, but Colt continued to use his single action design.

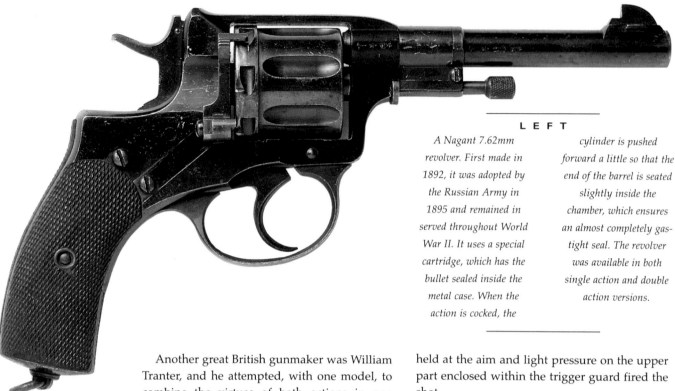

A Nagant 7.62mm revolver. First made in 1892, it was adopted by the Russian Army in 1895 and remained in served throughout World War II. It uses a special cartridge, which has the bullet sealed inside the metal case. When the action is cocked, the cylinder is pushed forward a little so that the end of the barrel is seated slightly inside the chamber, which ensures an almost completely gas-tight seal. The revolver was available in both single action and double action versions.

Another great British gunmaker was William Tranter, and he attempted, with one model, to combine the virtues of both actions in one system with his double trigger revolver. The trigger was longer than usual, and the end protruded through the guard. Pressure on this lower section rotated the cylinder and cocked the action. Once cocked the revolver could be held at the aim and light pressure on the upper part enclosed within the trigger guard fired the shot.

Other British makers produced percussion revolvers, and their names will be found stamped on the barrels or frames. Many enjoyed a comparatively short spell as manufacturers, but others achieved worldwide

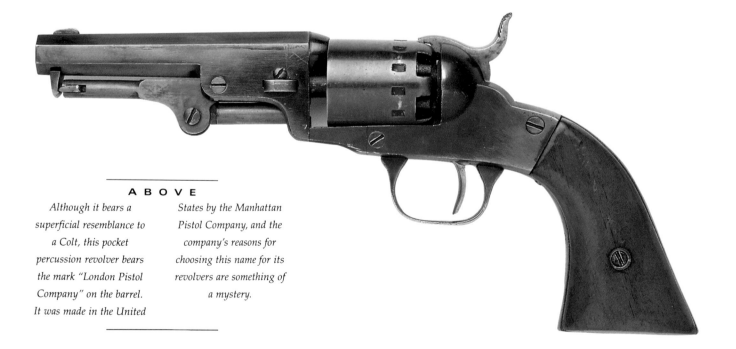

Although it bears a superficial resemblance to a Colt, this pocket percussion revolver bears the mark "London Pistol Company" on the barrel. It was made in the United States by the Manhattan Pistol Company, and the company's reasons for choosing this name for its revolvers are something of a mystery.

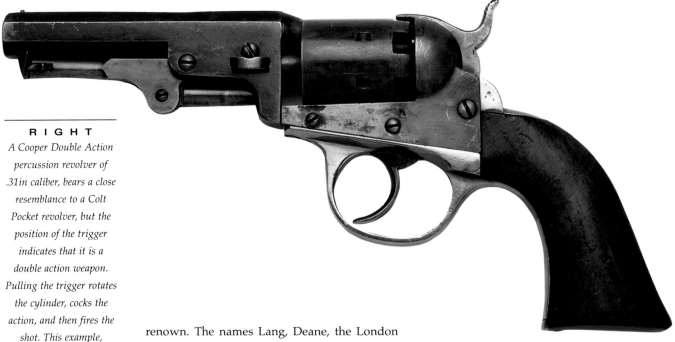

renown. The names Lang, Deane, the London Armoury Company, Baker, Daw, Harding, and W. Parker will all be found on a number of percussion revolvers, and that of Webley survived until well into this century.

British gunmakers were not the only manufacturers stirred by Colt's success, and in the United States there was an upsurge of revolver production stimulated by the Civil War. A variety of styles and patents was used, some blatantly copying Colt's products while others broke fresh ground. Firms such as Allen and Wheelock were in business only between 1857 and 1864 but supplied over 20 different model revolvers. The Bacon Manufacturing Company of Norwich, Connecticut, lasted from 1858 until 1867, producing percussion revolvers not dissimilar to Colt's Police Model.

Another Colt look-alike was produced by J. H. Cooper of Pittsburgh, Pennsylvania, but there was one very big difference for it had a double action mechanism, a feature revealed by the trigger, which requires a long pull and so sits further forwards inside the guard than the normal Colt style. Despite its name, the London Pistol Company was an American manufacturer, and the weapons were also made by the Manhattan Firearms Manufacturing Company.

An adventurous manufacturer was John Walch of New York City, who patented a system of 10- and 12-shot revolvers, but his output was small. In 1859 Alexandre Le Mat of New Orleans produced a percussion revolver, which had a shot barrel mounted below the normal pistol barrel. It was not a new idea and had been used by other makers some years before. The output of his weapons in America was limited, most of his revolvers being made in Europe. Many of the other names that first appeared around the mid-19th century were to fade rapidly, but others have survived and are still major producers today. Remington of Ilion, New York, was second only to Colt in the manufacture of revolvers and made over 14 different models. It is still producing firearms today.

During the Civil War the Confederate forces were very poorly supplied with manufacturing resources, but they did succeed in producing some revolvers. The Dance Brothers of Columbia, Texas, were probably the most prolific, but there were numerous other suppliers. There is a romantic air about the Southern forces, and weapons with Confederate markings are eagerly sought after—so much so that some unscrupulous dealers and collectors have obliged by marking them with CSA and similar markings. It is as well to be very cautious when offered Confederate weapons.

THE FIRST MODERN RIFLES

THE FIRST practical breech-loading sporting gun was developed in 1812 by Samuel Pauly, a Swiss gunsmith working in Paris. With a drop-down barrel and firing a self-contained cartridge, it was the father of the shotgun, and about 50 years ahead of its time. Indeed, it was so revolutionary that no military authorities took it seriously.

The needle gun was the brainchild of Johann Nikolaus von Dreyse, a Prussian gunsmith who, after his apprenticeship, traveled around Europe gaining experienced with various masters. Between 1809 and 1812 von Dreyse worked for Pauly, but by 1815 had returned to Prussia. There he began working on percussion muzzle-loaders, from which he progressed to developing a military breech-loader. In 1841 he offered his needle gun to the Prussian Army. Trials and modifications followed and the rifle was finally adopted as the infantryman's standard firearm in 1848.

BOLT-ACTION

The needle gun can justly be considered the ancestor of every bolt-action rifle, since it was the first weapon to feature the bolt system of closure. The bolt, resembling a common door-bolt, moved in a frame behind the rifle chamber. With the handle vertical the bolt could slide backward and forward to open and close the breech. Once the breech was closed, the handle was turned down in front of a lug in the frame to lock the bolt. The front end of the bolt was carefully coned to fit into the similarly coned breech opening, forming a gas-tight seal when the bolt was closed. The cartridge was a paper cylinder containing the bullet and powder charge, and the bullet carried a percussion cap on its base. The "needle" from which the gun derived its name was a long firing pin passing through the bolt. It was pulled back manually against a spring before the bolt was opened, and held by a catch. When the bolt was closed, pressing the trigger released the catch and caused the needle to pass right through the paper cartridge, striking the percussion cap and firing the round.

The bolt seal was effective when the weapon was new but it soon wore away and leaked gas. Nevertheless, the needle gun was broadly reliable, easy to use, and a potent weapon on the battlefield. It gave the Prussian infantry a rate of fire—perhaps eight rounds per minute—never known before and astonished the military world when it was first used in the Danish-Prussian war of 1864 and then in the Austro-Prussian war two years later.

On learning of the Prussian needle gun, the French immediately began developing their own version, the Chassepot rifle. Named after its inventor, a gunsmith at the Chatellerault arsenal, the gun appeared in 1863. It was, in fact, another bolt-action rifle, very similar to the needle gun but with a shorter firing pin. When used in conjunction with a paper and linen cartridge that carried a percussion cap in its end, the firing pin passed only a short way into the

BELOW
When the Prussian Army adopted the needle gun the details were carefully kept secret for many years. It was not until 1864 and its use against Denmark that its superiority became apparent. Nevertheless, it had two serious defects. First, the long needle-type firing pin, which passed entirely through the cartridge, was thus exposed to the explosion of the charge and corroded very quickly, leading to breakage in action. Second, the sealing of the bolt soon deteriorated so that flame from the cartridge often burned the firer's face. Men soon learned to fire a worn needle-gun from the hip not the shoulder.

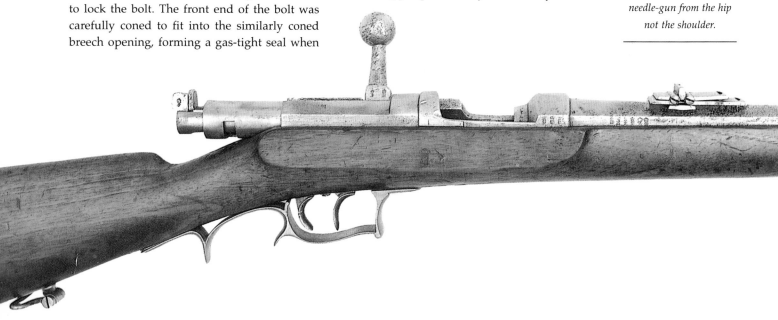

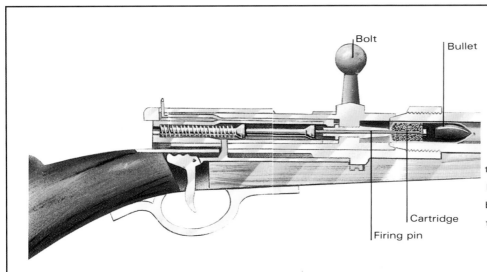

Bolt

Bullet

Cartridge

Firing pin

The father of all bolt-action rifles, the needle gun took its name from the long firing pin which passed through the paper cartridge to strike a cap in the base of the bullet. The explosion of the powder was confined by having the face of the bolt recessed and ground to a tight fit with the rear end of the barrel.

THE NEEDLE GUN

ABOVE

French troops engaged in a street fight with the Prussian forces during the Franco-Prussian war of 1870. The Chassepot rifled differed from the needle gun in not driving its firing pin entirely through the cartridge, and in having a more efficient rubber breech seal. The caliber was smaller, giving longer range, but the small bore was easily fouled.

Chassepot chamber before striking the cap and firing the round. The breech was sealed by an india-rubber ring around the head of the bolt. the pressure of the explosion pushed the bolt face back and squeezed the ring sideways to seal the chamber. However, the high temperature soon wore away the rubber, so each soldier carried a number of spare rings and was well drilled in changing them as soon as gas leaks occurred.

The Franco-Prussian War of 1870–1871 matched these two weapons against each other. During the fighting the Chassepot seemed to prove superior to the Dreyse needle gun; time and again the Prussians launched assaults on the French, only to come under such a withering fire outside the range of the needle gun that the attackers were either massacred or forced to give ground. However, subsequent tests on firing ranges have not confirmed the Chassepot's superiority.

The needle gun and the Chassepot proved conclusively that a breech-loader was better than a muzzle-loader, and signaled to the armies of the world that they should reequip with breech-loading small arms as soon as possible.

ALL PERCUSSION revolvers suffered from the same limitation—that is, of muzzle loading. Each chamber had to be filled with powder, a bullet rammed down on top of the powder and a cap placed on the nipple. Paper cartridges, which held one charge of powder, and a lead bullet were commonly used, but they still had to be torn open. There had been experiments with self-contained cartridges, and some had been very successful, although they had not been taken up for various reasons. However, the first really practical commercial steps were taken soon after the percussion principle had been adopted, and this was the system known as pinfire.

In 1835 the Frenchman Casimir Lefaucheux patented a system that used a metal or cardboard cartridge case with a small hole in the side through which a short metal pin passed. The tip of the rod rested on some fulminate embedded in the powder charge contained within the case. If this pin were struck, it pressed down to detonate the fulminate and so produce an explosive flash to ignite the charge. Lefaucheux designed guns with a small slot at the breech so that when the cartridge was inserted the pin could project through it, ready to be struck by the hammer.

The pinfire system was exhibited at the Great Exhibition in London in 1851, which Colt attended, but it seems to have attracted little attention despite the fact it now made breech-loading comparatively simple. Possibly because of the impetus given by Colt's display, in 1854

A B O V E

Typical of the cheaper form of firearm available in the latter part of the 19th century is this pinfire pepperbox revolver, which was made in Liège, Belgium. It consists of a cylinder, a simple butt, and a folding trigger, which operates a flat hammer. Such weapons, primarily intended for self-defense, are usually of small caliber, but this is of 7mm caliber.

Lefaucheux's son, Eugene, patented in France and Britain a revolver using the pinfire cartridge. Soon his firm was taking orders for military revolvers from several countries, including Egypt, as well as many civilian orders. Britain and the United States showed only limited interest, but on the continent of Europe pinfire

A B O V E

The long barrel on this .22in Smith & Wesson single shot pistol indicates that it is primarily a target weapon. It is a top break pistol and the first examples of this weapon were made on modified revolver frames but later the frame was altered. There were four main types produced although all are similar.

L E F T

Belgium, and especially the town of Liège, was an enormously busy center of production for a wide range of firearms. This is a particularly fine example of a pinfire revolver made there during the 19th century. A large quantity of guns was produced, and good examples can be acquired quite cheaply.

revolvers were produce in quantity and adopted by many countries for their armies. Some certainly saw service during the Civil War. Large numbers were manufactured for the civilian market and were often sold in cases with a range of accessories. Many revolvers were produced that had, as a safety measure, triggers that folded back to reduce the chances of snagging on clothing or a container.

The ease of loading a metal pinfire cartridge encouraged many European makers to design revolvers with large cylinders holding as many as 12 or 20 shots. A few had even more, although some became so bulky as to defeat their own purpose. Some makers, such as the French manufacturer Jarre, replaced the cylinder with a

flat bar drilled with chambers. Because of its shape, this is usually known as a harmonica gun.

Small revolvers composed of little more than the cylinder and a nominal barrel were fitted inside purses and small boxes, and one was combined with a folding knife and knuckle duster to make the so-called Apache pistol. Other small versions were mounted in walking sticks to offer a disguised self-defense weapon.

The majority of pinfire handguns were made in Belgium at the manufacturing town of Liège, and they may be easily recognized by the proof mark with the letters ELG, which are stamped into the frame and/or the cylinder.

R I G H T

This is a far less sophisticated single shot pistol typical of large numbers produced in Europe, especially in Belgium. It lacks a decent finish and can probably be best described as functional.

THE PINFIRE represented a significant step forward, but it had its limitations. The slot in the breech or chamber was a slight handicap, and the projecting pin representing a potential danger because an accidental knock could produce an unwanted shot. The system had, however, demonstrated the potential for the use of cartridges containing their own means of ignition. It was the far-sighted partnership of two famous names that made the next and crucial step. Horace Smith and Daniel Wesson, who were both from Massachusetts, were involved in the production of firearms, and in 1852 they joined forces and explored the possibilities of

the Hunt bullet, which had been patented in 1848. This was basically a lead bullet with a hollow base that was filled with propellant and covered by a disk with a central hole to allow ignition. The partners developed the idea and incorporated the concept of the Flobert cartridge, which was really only a percussion cap with a small lead ball pressed into the open end.

By 1856 Smith & Wesson had perfected the general design for a revolver that would take a metal cartridge loaded from the rear of the cylinder. They came to an agreement with an ex-employee of Colt, Rollin White, who had patented a revolver in which the chambers in the cylinder were drilled right through. This meant that the cartridge could be loaded from the rear. The cartridge had a small hollow rim, which held a deposit of fulminate, and when it was placed in the chamber the rim rested

RIGHT

It may look like a Colt Single Action Army revolver but it is a .22in version may by Ruger. This firm has become a very important manufacturer of weapons of excellent quality. This one has a floating firing pin which is mounted in the frame and not fitted to the hammer.

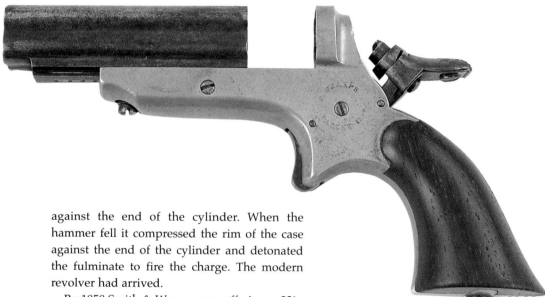

against the end of the cylinder. When the hammer fell it compressed the rim of the case against the end of the cylinder and detonated the fulminate to fire the charge. The modern revolver had arrived.

By 1858 Smith & Wesson was offering a .22in caliber breech-loading revolver for sale, and as they held the master patent no other gunmaker could copy the system without permission. The revolver was small, with the barrel hinged at the top and held closed by spring catches at the bottom of the cylinder housing. The cylinder was removable, and the empty cases could be pushed out using a rod fixed below the barrel. The weapon was well received but was somewhat limited in its appeal because of its small caliber—only .22in. In addition, the cases tended to swell when fired and sometimes jammed the action.

Increasing the caliber meant using a bigger case, but the metal could not be made too thick or the hammer could not crush it to detonate the charge. By 1861 Smith & Wesson had solved the problems and was offering a .32in revolver and working on designs for a .44in weapon.

THE ARRIVAL OF CENTER-FIRE

THE APPEARANCE of the Smith & Wesson revolvers established the basis of the modern handgun, but one further step was still necessary. Although the rimfire cartridge was a great improvement on previous loading sequences, it did have some limitations, especially when it was used for larger calibers. Two men were working, independently, toward the next big advance—in the United States, Colonel Berdan and in Britain, Colonel Edward Boxer. The outcome of their efforts in the 1860s was the center-fire cartridge. Instead of the fulminate compound being deposited in a thin layer over the inside base of the cartridge case, a percussion cap was fitted into a central hole in the base of the case. The walls and base of the case could now be of any thickness, since the only part to be hit was the cap. The design of the revolver hammer was changed so that it had a sharp point rather than the flat bar that had been used on the hammers of rimfire weapons—a useful guide in deciding whether a weapon is center-fire or pinfire. Detonation was swift and effective, and loading the cartridge was simple thanks to Rollin White's system.

Thus, by the 1860s, the style of almost every future revolver had been established, and the subsequent claims of manufacturers to have produced new models were accurate in only a limited sense.

There was still one problem to be resolved and that was how to insert the cartridges into the chambers of the cylinder. Three basic solutions were devised. On some revolvers, such as the Colt Single Action Army, a hinged plate was fitted to the frame just behind the butt end of the cylinder. To load the revolver, this plate or loading gate was flipped sideways to reveal the chambers awaiting the cartridges. The cylinder was rotated to expose each chamber for loading, and the gate was then closed. To extract the empty, fired cases the gate was opened, and some form of spring-loaded rod was fitted, usually below the barrel, which could be pushed back through the chamber to eject the case. Other revolvers used a similar system, but the loading gate hinged backward rather than sideways.

Another solution was to fit the cylinder onto a sideways swinging crane mounted in the

DIRECT
This .32in revolver with a five-shot cylinder was available in several forms, with square or bird's head butt and with spurred hammers. The manufacturer, Mervin Hulbert & Co., was active during the 1880s; most of its revolvers were nickel-plated.

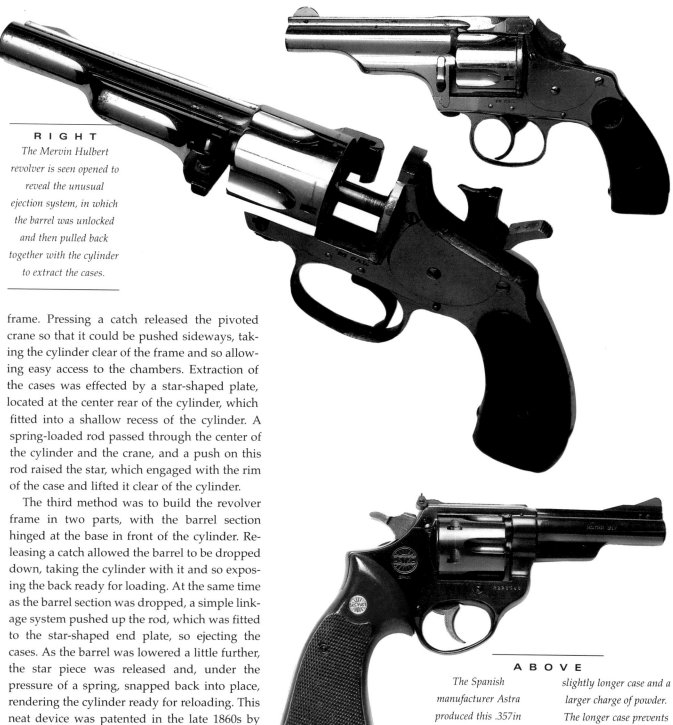

frame. Pressing a catch released the pivoted crane so that it could be pushed sideways, taking the cylinder clear of the frame and so allowing easy access to the chambers. Extraction of the cases was effected by a star-shaped plate, located at the center rear of the cylinder, which fitted into a shallow recess of the cylinder. A spring-loaded rod passed through the center of the cylinder and the crane, and a push on this rod raised the star, which engaged with the rim of the case and lifted it clear of the cylinder.

The third method was to build the revolver frame in two parts, with the barrel section hinged at the base in front of the cylinder. Releasing a catch allowed the barrel to be dropped down, taking the cylinder with it and so exposing the back ready for loading. At the same time as the barrel section was dropped, a simple linkage system pushed up the rod, which was fitted to the star-shaped end plate, so ejecting the cases. As the barrel was lowered a little further, the star piece was released and, under the pressure of a spring, snapped back into place, rendering the cylinder ready for reloading. This neat device was patented in the late 1860s by Smith & Wesson.

Because Smith & Wesson held the master patent for drilled-through cylinders, nobody could manufacture similar cylinders without their permission. There were numerous attempts to evade this restriction, and there were sundry odd law cases. However, in 1873 the master

A B O V E

The Spanish manufacturer Astra produced this .357in caliber revolver, which is available with various barrel lengths. The cartridge is a more powerful version of the .38in Special, which has a *slightly longer case and a larger charge of powder. The longer case prevents its being loaded into the cylinder of a .38in Special revolver, which might well fracture from the greater pressure of the more powerful charge.*

A B O V E

*Remington was
established in 1816 and is
still making guns today.
The company's
production of percussion
revolvers, one of which is
shown here, began in
1857, and it made a
variety of weapons
ranging from pocket
revolvers to large .44in
weapons for military use.*

patent expired and the field was open for all the gunmakers. The Colt factory then produced its best known weapon. Listed officially as the Colt Single Action Army Revolver, it retained the traditional Colt silhouette and had a 7½in (19.5cm) barrel, although other lengths were made. It had a loading gate at the rear of the cylinder, and a spring-loaded ejector rod was housed beneath the barrel. This weapon acquired a range of titles, including the six-shooter, the Equalizer and the Frontier. It was so popular and has become so enshrined in folk memory by its appearance in films, that it has remained almost continuously in production since 1873 and has been made in a wide assortment of calibers and barrel lengths. In films and on television it has featured at the Battle of the Alamo (1836) and in the Civil War (1861–1865)—a remarkable achievement for a weapon that was not made until 1873.

The armed services of most countries reviewed their weapons in the light of the latest developments, and the number of military revolvers that saw service is very high. The numbers

made obviously help to determine rarity, and some models are keenly sought after, but, on the other other hand, many military weapons saw plenty of service and tend to be somewhat worn and rubbed, which can depress their price.

In the United States a special group, the Small Arms and Accoutrements Board, was established to evaluate the needs of the army, and in 1870 it chose, surprisingly, a single-shot Remington pistol as well as a Smith & Wesson .44in caliber revolver. In 1873, however 8,000 Colt Single Action Army Revolvers in .45in caliber were purchased for the US Cavalry. A year later, in 1874, 3,000 Smith & Wesson Model 3 Schofield revolvers (so called after the officer who designed the original) were purchased, but generally the Colt seems to have been more popular with the troops.

In the 1878 model Colt deserted its long-established single action system and produced a double action revolver, but the US Army was not impressed. However, the double action system was here to stay, and many other revolver manufacturers adopted the system.

FASTER-LOADING RIFLES

After the various armies had satisfied their immediate needs by converting their muzzle-loading rifles into breech-loaders, the next move was to settle upon a properly designed breech-loading system, and by 1870 there was no shortage of those. Unfortunately, most of them were not robust enough for military service, and those that were had largely been designed for paper cartridges and were difficult to adapt to the new metallic cartridges.

The Civil War had accelerated the introduction of breech-loading into military circles with such weapons as the Sharps, Spencer, Burnside, Joslyn, and Starr carbines and rifles.

The Sharps used a vertically sliding breech block operated by a lever; the top edge was sharpened so as to slice the end off the paper cartridge as it closed, and it was fired by a hammer and percussion cap. The Starr used a linen cartridge and relied upon the force of the cap to pierce the linen and fire the powder. the Joslyn used a paper cartridge and closed the breech by a lifting flap carrying a gutta-percha seal. The Spencer and Burnside used metallic cartridges, the former a fairly ordinary rimfire, the latter a peculiar type which had to be loaded into the separate chamber base first before the weapon could be closed.

BELOW
The Snider breech-loading conversion of a British service rifle.

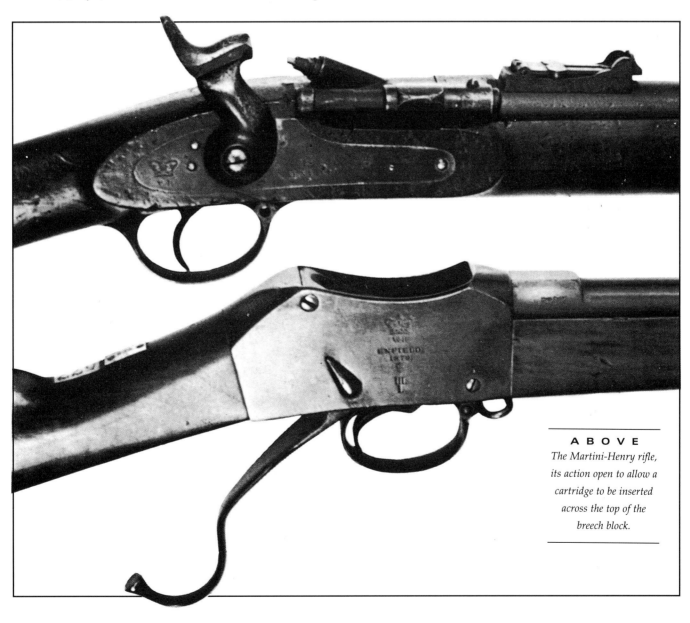

ABOVE
The Martini-Henry rifle, its action open to allow a cartridge to be inserted across the top of the breech block.

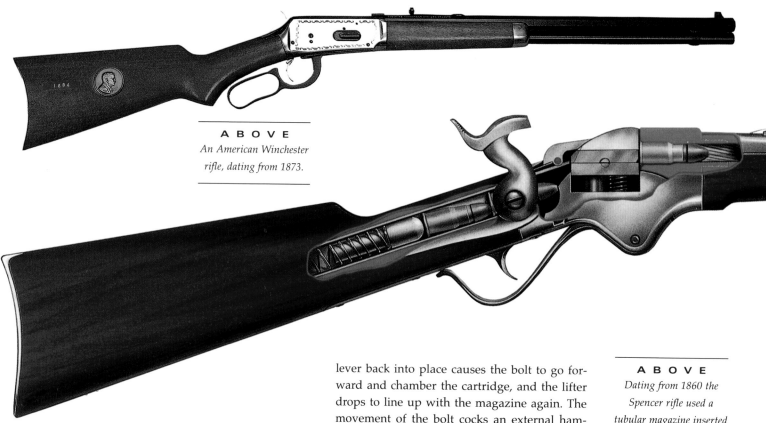

A B O V E
*An American Winchester
rifle, dating from 1873.*

THE WINCHESTER

The most famous of these "lever-action" designs was the Winchester. This began life as the "Volcanic" rifle, using an odd self-controlled round, which was simply a bullet with the base hollowed out to carry a powder charge and a cap. Its drawback was that the bullet had insufficient room to carry a charge sufficient to generate a worthwhile velocity and the gun's poor performance led to the company's bankruptcy in 1857. It was bought by Oliver Winchester, a haberdasher who knew little about guns but knew enough to hire a man who did—Benjamin T. Henry. He took the Volcanic and thoroughly redesigned it, adopting rimfire cartridges and later converting it to center-fire. In various forms the Winchester lever-action has remained in production ever since. The magazine is a tube running beneath the barrel; pushing down the lever unlocks and opens the bolt, then operates a "lifter" to carry a cartridge up from the magazine to the chamber. Lifting the

lever back into place causes the bolt to go forward and chamber the cartridge, and the lifter drops to line up with the magazine again. The movement of the bolt cocks an external hammer, which, when released, falls on to a firing pin in the bolt to fire the cartridge.

While these systems were adequate, none was sufficiently sound to attract interest from the major armies; the US Army, for example, settled on the Springfield conversion and stayed with it until 1892—by which time some very sophisticated systems were available. European armies, however, committed themselves to finding improved breech-loading systems and examined the various options available. Three types became popular—the rolling block, the falling block, and the bolt.

THREE BREECH-LOADING SYSTEMS

The rolling block system was perfected by Remington in the United States in 1864. Designed for a rimfire cartridge, it used a hinged block to close the breech; this block had a curved undersurface and behind it was the hammer, with a curved upper surface, so that as the hammer fell this surface passed beneath the block and securely supported it against the explosion of the cartridge. The Remington

A B O V E
Dating from 1860 the Spencer rifle used a tubular magazine inserted into the butt, feeding rimfire cartridges by a spring. Operating the under-lever rotated the breechblock back and picked up a cartridge from the tube; returning the lever chambered the cartridge and locked the breech. The external hammer then struck a firing pin in the breechblock.

This design by Frederick Prince (c.1855) incorporated a system tried by several inventors. The lever beneath the barrel was turned and pushed to unlock the barrel from the fixed breech-piece and then slid forward to expose the chamber. After loading, the barrel was pulled back and turned so that the lugs on the breech-piece engaged in the chamber and locked the barrel in place. This system proved too cumbersome in action to be practical.

system, in various calibers, was adopted by Sweden, Norway, Denmark, Spain, Greece, China, Egypt, and other countries.

The falling block was first developed by Henry Peabody of Boston in 1862. In this system the barrel was screwed into a rectangular box in which a solid breech block was pinned at its rear end. A lever beneath the weapon allowed this block to be swung down, exposing the mouth of the chamber, and a cartridge was inserted. Pulling up the lever raised the block to close the breech. The external hammer had to be cocked manually, and when released by the trigger it struck a curved firing pin in the block which in turn struck the rim of the cartridge and fired it. Peabody rifles were adopted by Canada, France, Bavaria, Mexico, and Switzerland.

In Switzerland Friedrich von Martini improved upon Peabody's idea by placing a firing pin and spring inside the breech block and arranging for it to be cocked as the opening lever

was operated. This did away with the need to cock the weapon as a separate action and also allowed the use of the system with center-fire cartridges. It was adopted by the British Army in 1871 as the "Martini-Henry" since it was combined with a barrel designed by Alexander Henry. The Martini system was also used by Turkey and Italy; Austria made some minor changes and adopted it as the Werndl rifle, and the Belgian Francotte-Martini was another of several variations.

The bolt system was developed extensively by Mauser, who set about improving the Chassepot rifle in the hope of interesting the French. His principal improvement was in adapting the idea to a cased cartridge and using a firing pin which was automatically cocked by the closing action of the bolt. The bolt had a prominent handle which was turned down in front of a lug on the receiver wall to lock the breech closed, and it was fitted at the rear with a safety catch which prevented the firing pin moving forward when applied.

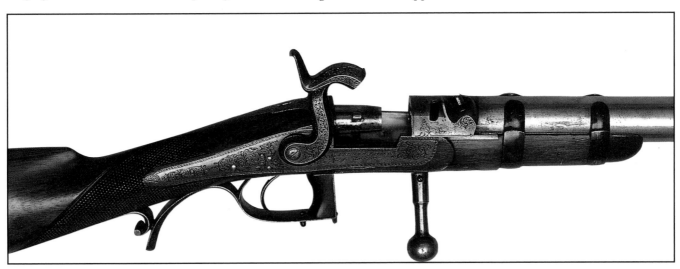

Magazine Rifle Advances

Having settled upon a particular breech-loading system (see pages 42–43), the armies of the world turned to considering the adoption of a magazine rifle, in order to give the individual soldier more firepower.

There were, of course, arguments against this; given a full magazine, said the opposition, the soldier will simply fire off all the ammunition as soon as he sees an enemy a mile away. But the siege of Plevna (1877) showed that this was not necessarily so. At Plevna the Turkish defenders, each with 500 rounds, were armed with Winchester magazine carbines, and they repulsed several Russian attacks with withering, disciplined firepower. This showed that any army without a magazine rifle was at a disadvantage.

Despite its success at Plevna, the American Winchester was rarely used as a military weapon; but it introduced the tubular magazine, in which a row of ammunition was carried in a tube beneath the barrel. Individual rounds were pushed back by a spring and fed up to the chamber by working a lever that also cocked the hammer. This was satisfactory with soft-nosed bullets, but the small-caliber jacketed bullets that the military were contemplating using risked firing the cap of the next cartridge in front under the shock of recoil, and accordingly the tubular magazine was not trusted.

Nevertheless, the French adopted the tubular magazine for their 8-mm Lebel rifle (1886), as did the Germans for their Commission rifle (1888), since it provided a quick solution.

THE BOLT-ACTION RIFLE

James Paris Lee, a Scot who emigrated to the United States, had developed a bolt-action rifle. Beneath the bolt was a metal box, into which cartridges were placed on top of a spring. As the bolt was opened, the spring forced the cartridges up against a stop; the bolt pushed the top cartridge into the chamber as it closed. After firing, the opening of the bolt extracted the empty cartridge case, and the return stroke loaded a fresh round. The box could be detached for refilling, and the rifle was provided with a spare magazine for quick reloading in action. Lee had produced a few sporting rifles on this principle, and after severe testing, the Lee bolt and magazine were adopted by the British Army in the Lee-Metford rifle, Metford being the designer of the barrel. Another innovation was the adoption of a jacketed bullet of .303-in caliber, a considerable reduction from the .45 caliber which was usual for military rifles of the day.

The small jacketed bullet was developed by Major Rubin of the Swiss Army. It had high velocity (giving better accuracy) and, due to its metal jacket, did not leave a coating of lead in the rifle barrel. The French took the same course, though using a solid brass bullet, with

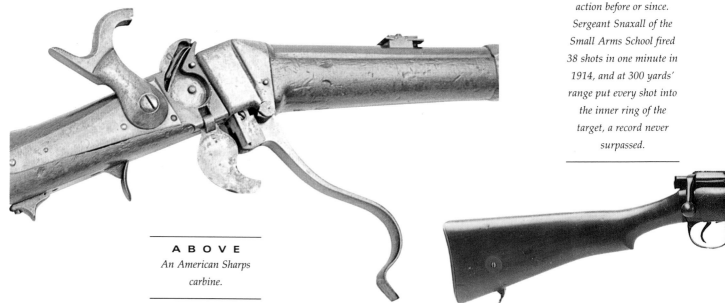

A B O V E
An American Sharps carbine.

their M1886 rifle, as did the Germans with their M1888 rifle.

The Germans realized that their tubular magazine weapon had been a mistake, and applied to Mauser for something better. He adapted the box magazine idea and produced a rifle with a five-shot box magazine concealed inside the stock. The rifle's bolt action was improved, locking into the chamber of the barrel, and the Mauser rifles developed in the 1890s were to be exported throughout the world.

In Austria, Count Mannlicher designed another magazine rifle, similar in some respects to the Mauser but eventually adopting a "straight-pull" bolt and a rotating magazine, still concealed inside the butt. The straight-pull bolt relied upon cam action: the bolt handle was pulled straight back, withdrawing a sleeve which drew a stud through a curved cam path in the bolt body, causing it to rotate. Some people said it was quicker than a turn-bolt, but it was generally more fragile. the Swiss adopted a straight-pull design, while the Japanese and Italians copied Mauser. Only the Scandinavians and the Americans tried something different, in the Krag-Jorgensen rifle, which had an odd side-mounted magazine fed through a trapdoor.

Other countries adopted various bolt action weapons; the United States took the Krag-Jorgensen, which had a side-feeding magazine; Russia adopted the Mosin-Nagant, a Belgian design that was fairly unremarkable, as was the

The Lebel mechanism
The mechanism of the bolt-action Lebel rifle, showing how the ammunition lies in the tubular magazine beneath the barrel. The bolt is closed, with a round ready to be fired, and the cartridge lifter is down, ready to lift the next cartridge after it has been pushed onto the lifter by a spring.

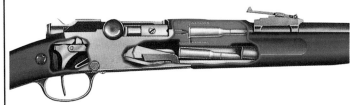

The Lee bolt mechanism
A sectioned drawing of the Lee action; the bolt has just been opened, extracting the empty case. The simple trigger mechanism, and the folded spring which forces the cartridge up in front of the bolt as it closes can be seen.

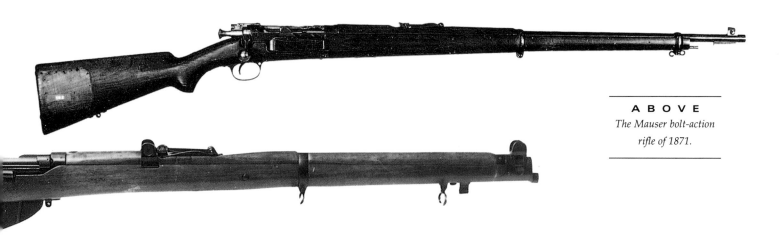

ABOVE
The Mauser bolt-action rifle of 1871.

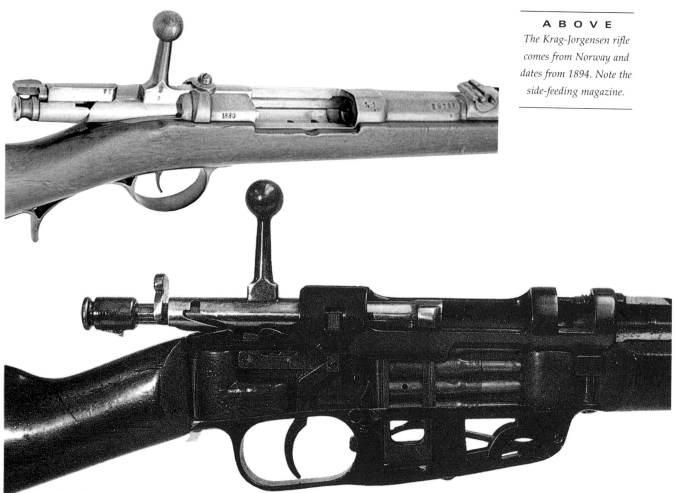

Japanese Arisaka and the Italian Carcano. The German Army returned to Mauser in 1898 and adopted his "Gewehr 98," the ultimate Mauser with which they stayed until 1945. The only major step to be taken was the British adoption of the Lee-Enfield system; this used the same bolt action and magazine as before, but now allied to a new barrel developed by the Royal Small Arms Factory at Enfield. This was the result of the British adoption of cordite smokeless powder; this demanded a somewhat different system of rifling to get the best performance out of the weapon.

Hitherto, the infantry had been provided with long rifles, while the cavalry, artillery, engineers and others, who merely needed a defensive weapon, had been given short carbines. As now seems obvious, this was uneconomic, since it meant producing several different weapons (because the cavalry simply could not have the same carbine as the engineers), to-

gether with all the spares and maintenance problems involved. The "Short Magazine Lee-Enfield" was accordingly developed. Shorter than the long rifle, longer than the carbine, it became the universal issue, an idea that was rapidly followed by the United States (which abandoned the Krag and adopted the Springfield, a modified Mauser design) and Germany. The SMLE also introduced charger loading to the British, using five-round chargers to load the ten-round magazine of the Lee-Enfield.

Broadly speaking, bolt actions have changed very little during the 20th century. The British L42A1 7.62mm sniping rifle in use today is the same Lee-Enfield action that was introduced in 1903 on the SMLE, with a few very small changes to simplify production, while the Federal German Army's Mauser 66SP sniping rifle uses the same 1898 Mauser action, again slightly improved over the years.

COLT'S RIVALS AND SUCCESSORS

IN BRITAIN the principal revolver design was produced by Robert Adams in 1851; this was a solid-frame weapon, inherently stronger than Colt's open frame, and the firing mechanism was self-cocking—pulling the trigger raised and then dropped the hammer. By contrast Colt's revolver employed a single action, in which the hammer had to be manually cocked and then released by the trigger. Adams's and Colt's designs competed for many years for military approval, both being adopted by various forces; the general opinion was that the Colt had the advantage in accuracy, the Adams in speed of operation.

When Colt's master patent expired in 1857, there was a rush of competitors with designs roughly based on the Colt, but these were all percussion weapons. Horace Smith and Daniel Wesson, looking to the future, patented a rim-fire cartridge in 1854 and acquired another mas-

LEFT

The British Enfield .476in B.L. revolver was designed in 1879 and tested by various units of the British Army. After a somewhat mixed reception, it was modified slightly before being adopted as the official revolver in August 1880. Service use revealed more problems, and the design was further modified. The Mark II shown here was eventually adopted in 1887.

ABOVE

The extraction system of the Enfield revolver is remarkable. When the barrel catch was released and the barrel pushed downward, the cylinder moved forwards, but a stationary plate retained the cases so that, eventually, there was sufficient room for the empty case to fall out.

ter patent covering any cylinder with chambers bored through from end to end. In 1857 they went into production with a 0.22in caliber rimfire-cartridge revolver and, thanks to their patent, enjoyed a virtual monopoly in the United States until 1869.

A number of Colt percussion revolvers were ordered by the British Army in 1856, and Navy Colts stamped with the broad arrow indicating official-issue weapons are sought after by collectors today. In 1868 the British Army changed to breech-loading weapons, and many of the Adams and Colt percussion weapons were adapted to take a Boxer center-fire cartridge. As late as 1872 many units of the British Army were still being issued with single-shot percussion pistols, but after long discussions and some obstruction from the Duke of Cambridge, the Commander-in-Chief, revolvers were authorized for the Lancer units in 1877. Officers were always free to purchase their own revolvers, so that there was always a variety of weapons in service.

In August 1880 the pistol revolver B.L. Enfield (Mark 1), which fired a .45in cartridge, was officially approved for British Army use. This was a break revolver—that is, when a catch at the top was released the barrel could be depressed and the star plate remained stationary in the rear position just far enough forward for the empty case to fall clear, while any unfired cartridges, being longer, stayed in position. These revolvers were not very popular, and a number of changes were made, including the addition of a safety catch, which is very unusual in revolver technology. These revolvers are still not uncommon, and because they are not greatly sought after they sell very

A B O V E

This is a Belgian-made 11mm version of the Gasser revolver. These weapons were designed by the Austrian Leopold Gasser in 1869, and they saw service with the *armies of the Austro-Hungarian Empire. This example is in the Montenegrin style, and such models are comparatively common since the king of* *Montenegro ordered all his male subjects to purchase an example. Most are crudely decorated and have grips of horn or mother-of-pearl.*

A B O V E

The Webley .455/.476 W.G. Army Revolver, which was produced in slightly different forms between 1886 and c.1902. A solid weapon, intended *primarily for military service, it was adapted for target shooting. The 6in (15cm) barrel was well suited for accuracy and high-quality action.*

A B O V E

A close-up of the Gasser revolver, showing the simple, side-mounted ejector rod, which was *used to push out the empty cases when the plate at the rear of the cylinder was pushed clear.*

reasonably at auction. Many have seen hard service, however, and may not be in very good condition.

In 1886 the famous British name of Webley made its mark on the official revolver field when a revolver produced by the company was adopted by the Royal Irish Constabulary. It was a rugged, sturdy weapon, firing a .442in cartridge, and it saw service with many police forces of the Empire, including those in Australia and South Africa. In 1887 the Webley Pistol (Mark I) was made the official revolver of the British Army. It was a .441in caliber and had a 4in (10cm) barrel with a top beak. This was a reliable and sturdy weapon, and some 10,000 were ordered. This was but the first of a long line of Webley revolvers in various styles and calibers to be issued to the British Army, and some saw service during World War II.

All European nations examined their armament provision in the light of the changes that had taken place, and Belgium's arms center at Liège was kept extremely busy producing revolvers for Belgium's own army and for many others as well. One easily recognizable product was the Gasser revolver, which was made for Montenegro, a small Balkan state. Most of these are massive and have what looks like a disproportionately small butt.

THE WEBLEY-FOSBERY

An unusual British revolver was designed by Colonel George Fosbery and made by Webley. The Webley-Fosbery was a self-cocking revolver in which the recoil drove back the upper section of the weapon, including the cylinder. As it moved back, a stud engaged with a zigzag groove cut into the face of the cylinder. This turned the cylinder and brought the next chamber in line with the barrel and at the same time cocked the action. The six shots could be fired as rapidly as the trigger could be pulled, and accuracy was helped by the fact that only a light pressure was needed to operate the trigger. It was an accurate weapon but expensive to produce, and although it saw service in South Africa during the Boer War (1899–1902), it had been more or less forgotten by World War II.

LEFT
The Webley .455in Revolver Mark II, which was approved for service in May 1895, differed in only minor details from the Mark I. The butt has a smoother outline, and the hammer is a little more robust. There were other, less obvious modifications, and this example is shown in the "open" position, with the self-extractor ready to extract the empty cases.

LEFT

A Galand revolver with the barrel and cylinder in the forward position, ready for case extraction. This model was adopted by the Russian Navy in 1870, and examples with Russian markings may be found. They are not common, and their rather unusual system makes them of special interest to collectors.

RIGHT

Although the name Smith & Wesson immediately suggests an American weapon, this example was made by that firm primarily for Russia. The company was contracted to supply thousands of revolvers for the Russian armed forces, and Turkey later placed a contract for a thousand Second Model Russian revolvers. Surprisingly, they were intended to take the .44in Henry rimfire cartridge.

Another very recognizable revolver manufactured in Liège is the Galand, which was designed by a Frenchman and adopted by the Russian Navy. The distinguishing feature is the trigger guard, which extends forward under the barrel. Unlocked by a small catch, it swings forward and down, moving the entire barrel assembly forward. The cartridges pass through a plate at the rear of the cylinder, and this also moves forward a short distance and then stops, but the cylinder continues to move forward. The distance is such that empty cases are pulled clear of the cylinder but the unfired cartridges, which are longer because the bullets are *in situ*, remain in place. Returning the trigger guard to the closed position replaces the plate and makes the cylinder ready for action.

The Russians also adopted a Smith & Wessen revolver, the Model 3, Russian First Model, which was slightly modified to take the Russian .44in cartridge. A Second Model was issued later, and this has as spur extending down from the trigger guard to provide a firmer grip. Later, some of the revolvers were made in Berlin and in Tula, the center of Russian arms manufacture.

In 1895 the Russians changed to a smaller caliber weapon, the Nagant gas seal revolver. this weapon, which was designed by a Frenchman, is very unusual in that the bullet is totally enclosed within the metal case and the neck is slightly tapered. When it is loaded the tip of the cartridge projects slightly beyond the end of the cylinder. If the action is cocked the entire cylinder is pushed forward, which means that the tip of the cartridge engages with the barrel. The idea was that in normal revolvers there has to be a slight gap between the end of the cylinder and the mouth of the barrel through which there was a considerable leakage of gas when a shot was fired. The Nagant system sealed the gap and prevented the loss of pressure. There was a single action version of the Nagant, which was issued to noncommissioned officers, and a double action model for officers. The Norwegian Army also issued it to its troops.

One of the largest and, to many, the ugliest military revolvers is the German Reichsrevolver with its big curving butt and, for a revolver, large safety catch. It was awkward to load, but this was probably because the German Army regarded handguns as inferior weapons, to be used only in dire emergencies or by charging cavalry.

Commercial Guns Shooting as a sport was gaining in popularity, and there was a continuing growth in small bore, .22in, revolvers. Numerous companies supplied the target shooting market, particularly in the United States. Their output was considerable, and Iver Johnson of New Jersey and Harrington & Richardson Inc. of Massachusetts made thousands of small bore revolvers, most of which were top-break models with automatic ejection of the empty cases. Some manufacturers, including Smith & Wesson, Stevens, and Webley, produced single-shot target guns, many of which had longer barrels to improve accuracy. They are almost invariably single action to ensure a steady grip and easy firing, for with this action much less pressure is required to operate the trigger, and consequently the revolver is less likely to turn in the hand as the

trigger is pressed. Some makers also supplied conversion sets so that a full bore revolver could be converted to fire the smaller .22in caliber. They usually include an alternative cylinder and a rifled tube, which could be inserted into the fixed-barrel to reduce the bore.

Another fruitful market was for what might be called self-defense weapons. These were gen-

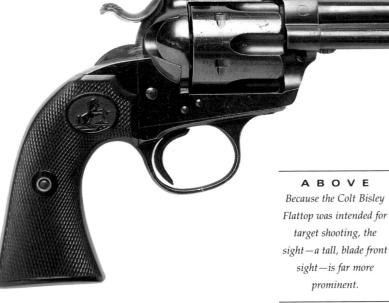

erally small revolvers with a caliber of .22in or .25in and small enough to drop into a pocket. There were two main types, which differed in the hammer fitting. The usual type had a spur on the hammer so that it could be cocked manually. This could snag on clothing and possibly cock the action or even fire the revolver accidentally. The solution was the hammerless model. Yet another solution was to enclose the hammer within two shielding walls, with perhaps just the tip showing so that it was possible, but not easy, to cock the action manually.

SMOKELESS POWDER AND BEYOND

SELF-LOADING PISTOLS only became a realistic proposition after the invention of smokeless propellants at the end of the 19th century. Until then, the debris and acid residues left after firing a black powder cartridge soon fouled the intricate moving parts of the (then) experimental semiautomatic handguns. The principal components of smokeless powders, however, are created by the action of nitric acid on organic chemicals or fibers, which produces nitroglycerine and forms of nitrocellulose such as guncotton, both of which date from the middle of the 1800s. A Prussian inventor named Shultze made a black powder substitute from nitrated wood in 1865 that achieved limited success. Most of the new propellants could not be used, however, until a simple method of stabilizing them was found by Nobel in the 1870s.

BASIC PRINCIPLES

The basic principle of all self-loading firearms is the same. By utilizing either gas produced when fired, or the recoil energy generated by the round, a spent cartridge case is ejected from the breech and a fresh round of ammunition inserted from a magazine. The vast majority of self-loading pistols also recock the hammer or striker when cycling. Early military self-loading pistols were single-action only, the hammer needing to be manually cocked before firing. The cocking usually took place as the slide was racked to chamber a round, then a safety catch would be applied. Modern self-loading pistols of up to 9mm Luger and .45 ACP calibers frequently have a double-action trigger, where a pull on the trigger will cock and fire the gun, and subsequent shots are fired with the hammer cocked by the automatic cycling of the action on firing. There have been a small number of trigger-cocked-only self-loading pistols available, with Smith & Wesson now proposing to offer the facility on its range of self-loaders.

The self-loading action itself occurs in any one of the following ways:

Blowback Straight blowback is the simplest self-loading system used for pistols. It is used on most low-powered pistols of caliber 9mmK (.380 Auto) and below. The breech holds the cartridge in the chamber by spring pressure. When fired the spring and the inertia of the breech block keep the breech closed until the bullet has traveled most of the way down the normally short barrel, or indeed left it. The breech block, in the form of a slide or bolt, then moves back under recoil, opening the breech. A hooked extractor pulls the spent cartridge out and backward with the breech block until the rim of the case hits an ejector, which knocks it out through an ejection part. On the forward travel under spring pressure the breech block picks up another round from the magazine and pushes it into the chamber ready for the next shot. Straight blowback is not used for more powerful calibers as either the recoil spring would need to be very strong, or a very large breech-block with a great deal of inertia would be required to keep the action closed during firing. This system is used successfully on machine pistols where weight is not such a problem.

Delayed blowback For higher-powered ammunition the breech of a self-loading pistol needs to be kept positively closed until the bullet has left the barrel and the chamber pressure has dropped. To achieve this a delayed blowback action of some sort must be used. The most common method is the short recoil Browning locked breech design invented by firearms genius John Moses Browning and first patented in 1897. When the slide and breech are fully forward in battery, the barrel is pushed up by a swinging link and lugs on the barrel engage with slots in the slide. On firing, the barrel and breech remain locked and start to recoil backwards together. As the gas pressure drops, the barrel cams down on the swinging link, allowing the slide to travel fully rearward, extracting the spent case and rechambering a new one, like a straight blowback pistol. The first design used two links, one at each end of the barrel, but this was later refined into a single link version for a pistol that was made by Colt and adopted by the US Army in 1911. The Model 1911 pistol fired a new powerful cartridge, .45 Automatic Colt Pistol (.45 ACP), and it remained the US military issue sidearm until it was replaced by the 9mm Luger caliber Beretta 91 series pistols in the 1980s. After his death, Browning's design was further refined by Fabrique Nationale in Belgium and in 1935 they produced the GP35

pistol in 9mm Luger which used an angled lug on the underside of the barrel to produce the same locked breech and delayed blowback effect. The other main delayed blowback design still common today is the Walther/Beretta wedge system where a pivoting wedge on the underside of the barrel and slide lock together under the pressure of the gas in the chamber. After recoiling a short distance together the barrel and slide are unlocked by a sliding pin at the rear of the locking wedge. By this time the pressure in the chamber has dropped, and the wedge drops down permitting the slide to move backward.

Gas-operated pistols There have been many unsuccessful attempts to make gas-operated self-loading pistols. They have generally been bulky and complex requiring a powerful cartridge to cycle the action. The breech is usually held shut by a rotating bolt on the slide which locks into lugs in the chamber. Gas is tapped off from the barrel or chamber during firing and pushes against a piston connected to the slide. As in delayed blowback designs, the breech remains closed until the chamber pressure drops and the pistol force on the slide causes the bolt to unlock and the slide to cycle the action. The Wildey pistol is still produced using this system as is the Israeli Desert Eagle with which it competes as the world's most powerful production self-loading pistol.

"Automatic" and self-loading revolvers There have been some notable attempts to produce self-loading, self-cocking or "automatic" revolvers too, the most famous being the British Webley-Fosbery made between 1901 and 1914. A 6-shot revolver similar in appearance to the self-extracting Webley .455 caliber Mark VI, the

A B O V E
.45 ACP has an enviable reputation as a powerful sporting and defense cartridge. Smith & Wesson make stainless steel double-action pistols to fire it. The full size Model 4506 (direct) has a magazine capacity of eight rounds, the compact Model 4516's magazine holds seven plus one in the chamber.

Fosbery used the recoil energy of the fired round to index the cylinder and recock the hammer. The Fosbery was the most successful of the line of "automatic" revolvers that had been made at various times throughout the world. One of the earliest was the Spanish Orbea system of 1863, which had a gas port in the barrel and a gas piston, a mechanism frequently found on modern self-loading rifles. In the Orbea revolver a series of levers rotated the cylinder and extracted the fired case. The Paulsen revolver of 1866 also used a gas piston which cocked the hammer and indexed the cylinder.

ADVANTAGES

Apart from the very first models produced, self-loading pistols offered a number of advantages over the revolver. They could hold more ammunition, usually in a detachable clip magazine. The clip magazine meant that they could be reloaded very quickly by replacing an empty magazine with a charged one. Also, felt recoil from a pistol is generally lower than that of a revolver of the same weight using the same energy ammunition. Some of the recoil is absorbed in the cycling of the action and the pistol can be held closer to the line of the bore reducing the torque during firing. Without a bulky revolving cylinder, pistols are much slimmer than wheel-guns, and without the cylinder to barrel gap, little or none of the propellant combustion gas is wasted.

DISADVANTAGES

There are disadvantages to the pistol as well. A revolver is far quicker to reload from loose rounds and is more reliable with a wide range of ammunition. For a pistol, the ammunition quality has to be consistent otherwise it will fail to extract or to feed. If a cartridge fails to fire for some reason, or there is another malfunction, two hands are usually needed to clear the jam. If a revolver misfires, the action can be thumb-cocked or trigger-cocked with one hand to bring a fresh cartridge in line with the bore. In the past, revolver actions could generally cope with far higher powered ammunition than a pistol, due to the size of the rounds and the stresses on the reciprocating parts limiting the power of the

self-loader. This difference, however, has been whittled down in more recent years.

The double-action revolver became the preferred handgun for law enforcement and civilian personal defense, and it is only recently that American and British police forces have started to employ the self-loading pistol in preference to the revolver.

MILITARY SPECIALIZATION

Military forces started adopting the self-loading pistol at the turn of the century, having provided the original impetus for its development along with self-loading rifles and automatic machine-guns. Armies have the resources to specify and check the performance of their ammunition, and because "skill at arms" training is part of their daily schedule, the drawbacks of self-loading pistols diminish. In any event the handgun is usually regarded as a last resort personal defensive weapon for soldiers who prefer artillery and assault rifles as their main firepower. Certain special forces units use handguns offensively for counterterrorist operations and for hostage release actions at short ranges where machine pistols and rifles are too bulky.

BELOW
Ruger's new P85 pistol uses a swinging link to effect delayed blowback, just like John Browning did in his original Colt 1911.

BIRTH OF THE AUTOMATIC

THE HONOR of developing effective automatic arms goes to an Austrian named Laumann, who had patented a mechanical bolt action pistol and then converted it into a delayed blowback weapon. He had a small number—fewer than 100 of these pistols made by the Steyr-Mannlicher factory and marketed as the "Schonberger" pistol in 1892—though at this late date we cannot say who Schonberger was—probably Laumann's financial backer. It was in 8mm caliber; only one is now known to exist, and nobody now living has ever seen a round of the ammunition, but it was undoubtedly the first production automatic pistol.

BORCHARDT AND LUGER

The following year saw the arrival of a design destined to become a legend. Hugo Borchardt emigrated to America in the 1860s and became a US citizen. He worked for some time with Winchester designing revolvers, but none of his designs were produced and Borchardt returned to Europe to work for the Hungarian arsenal. There, he saw a demonstration of Maxim's machine gun and began thinking about an automatic pistol as a result. He adopted Maxim's toggle lock, so that as the pistol barrel recoiled, the lock folded up to withdraw the bolt, simultaneously winding up a clock-type spring. He also pioneered the use of a box magazine in the butt plus developing the vital factor—the 7.63mm rimless necked cartridge—without which the design could not have worked. The result was the Borchardt pistol, made by Ludwig Loewe in Berlin and launched on the market in 1893. It is believed that about 3,000 Borchardt pistols were made between 1893 and 1896, and it was certainly the first automatic pistol to sell in quantity. It was a cumbersome design, with a fragile and easily dislocated mechanism, but Borchardt seemed satisfied with it and, apart from patenting some minor improvements, which he never actually incorporated into the design, he left it and went on to other things.

It was left to another Loewe employee, Georg Luger, to take the Borchardt and turn it into a more practical weapon. He cleaned up the design, placing the return spring in the butt, and developed a somewhat powerful 7.65mm

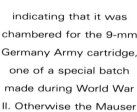

The Mauser c/96, or "Military" model, has a unique appearance, with the magazine ahead of the trigger and the peculiar "broomhandle" grip, but it was made like a fine watch, not a single screw or pin being used in its assembly except to hold the wooden grips in place. This model has a "9" carved into the butt, indicating that it was chambered for the 9-mm Germany Army cartridge, one of a special batch made during World War II. Otherwise the Mauser was always in 7.63mm caliber.

cartridge. He also changed the angle of the grip, so that the pistol pointed more instinctively and lay more comfortably in the hand. The result was the Luger pistol—properly called the Parabellum pistol—which appeared in 1900. It was adopted by the Swiss in 1901, but the German Army wanted something of a heavier caliber, and Luger therefore took the 7.65mm cartridge, opened out the mouth and inserted a 9mm bullet. It was to remain the official German pistol until the beginning of World War II.

One reason for Luger's development of his pistol was the fact that the sales of the Borchardt had suffered from competition with Mauser, who produced his own superior automatic in 1896. The Mauser used the Borchardt cartridge, though it was renamed the 7.63mm Mauser cartridge in this connection. The pistol employed a recoiling bolt locked by lugs underneath it and unlocked by short recoil of the barrel and frame. The magazine was in front of the trigger, like the Mauser rifle, it was loaded through the open action by using a charger of ten cartridges. In common with the Borchardt, it was given a wooden butt, which clipped to the pistol's grip to make a rudimentary carbine. It was accurate, robust, and beautifully made and sold well; but it failed to attract the German Army and,

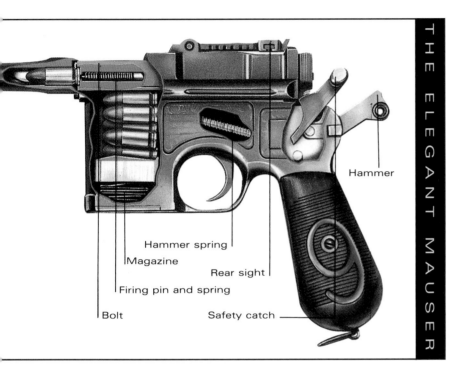

THE ELEGANT MAUSER

Hammer

Hammer spring

Magazine

Rear sight

Firing pin and spring

Bolt

Safety catch

indeed, was rarely the official service pistol for any major force, though it was widely purchased independently by many officers.

Two other European designs of this period deserve mention. Theodor Bergmann employed a talented designer, Louis Schmeisser, to develop a simple blowback weapon, adapting the principle that the Skoda machine gun had pioneered. It was rather like the Mauser in layout, with a clip-fed magazine in front of the trigger, but the cartridge was a low-powered 6mm. The weapon was cheap, simple, and sold well. Schmeisser went on to develop locked-breech designs in the hopes of a military contract and eventually succeeded in 1905, with a 9mm pistol which the Spanish Army adopted.

Unfortunately Bergmann's manufacturing facilities were small, so he had to contract out work on the pistol. His subcontractor was taken over by a larger firm, which then canceled the contract and left Bergmann with no means of

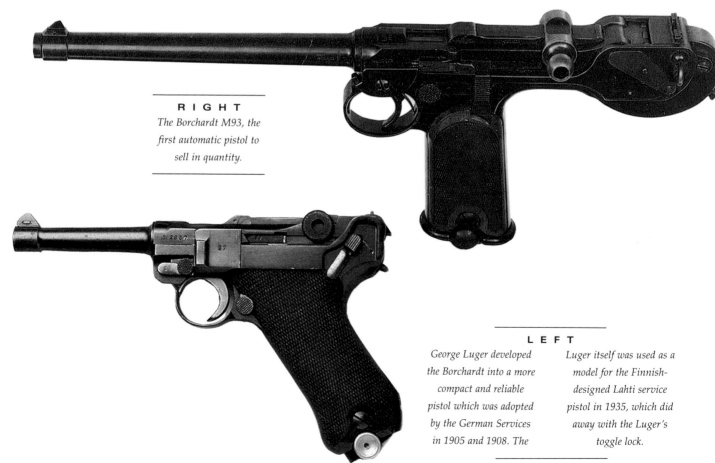

R I G H T
The Borchardt M93, the first automatic pistol to sell in quantity.

L E F T
George Luger developed the Borchardt into a more compact and reliable pistol which was adopted by the German Services in 1905 and 1908. The
Luger itself was used as a model for the Finnish-designed Lahti service pistol in 1935, which did away with the Luger's toggle lock.

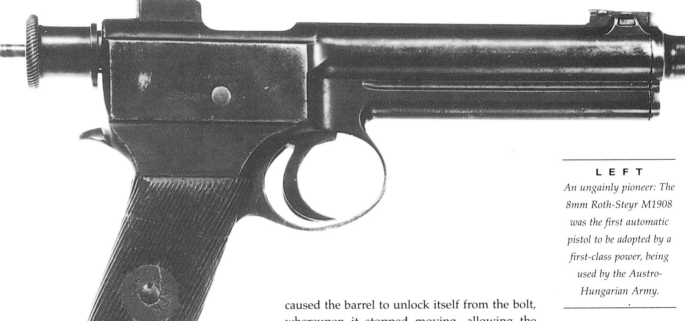

production. He sold the contract to Pieper, a Belgian company, and retired from the pistol business. Pieper renamed the weapon the Bergmann-Bayard (Bayard being their trademark) and completed the Spanish contract, then obtained another to supply the Danish Army.

In 1907 the Austro-Hungarian Army became the first major army to adopt an automatic pistol (a year before the Germans), when they approved the Roth-Steyr. This was a complex weapon, which adopted an entirely new method of locking the breech. The barrel was free to revolve inside an enveloping sleeve; behind it, was the bolt, also enclosed in the sleeve, which formed the body of the pistol. At the front of the barrel were two helical lugs, which engaged in grooves in the inner surface of the sleeve. When the barrel recoiled, locked to the bolt, it pulled these lugs along the slots, which turned the barrel through about 30 degrees; this

caused the barrel to unlock itself from the bolt, whereupon it stopped moving, allowing the bolt to continue rearward, extract the empty case and then, driven by a spring move forward to load the next round. An odd feature was that the magazine, though in the grip, was loaded through the top of the weapon by opening the bolt and then using a charger of ten rounds and driving them down into the magazine. It was also odd in that the firing pin was only partially cocked as the weapon reloaded; full cocking involved pulling the trigger, which first completed the cocking of the firing pin and then released it. It is said that this was insisted upon by the military because the pistol was for issue to cavalry and they were afraid of what might happen if a trooper had his finger on the trigger of a cocked pistol if his horse suddenly became skittish.

THE "ORIGINAL BROWNING"

In the United States the automatic pistol had a hard time finding a home. John Browning developed a simple blowback pistol in .32 caliber, a cartridge he had developed especially for it. He was unable to find an American manufacturer and took the design to Europe, where he arranged with the Fabrique Nationale d'Armes de Guerre of Liège, Belgium, to manufacture his designs. Using the name "Browning," they subsequently produced his blowback pistols by the million. His first model became known as the "Original Browning" or the Model 1900, and he soon followed it with an even simpler model. This became the Model 1903, one of the simplest and most successful pistol designs ever made. However, the cartridge was not sufficiently powerful for military use, so Browning went back to his design office to develop a locked breech pistol capable of firing a heavy load. This time, there was a more receptive atmosphere at home and the Colt company took up his military design. It took several years to perfect it but finally, in 1911, the Colt .45 automatic pistol became the standard US sidearm. It was to hold this position for the next 70 years, one of the longest-lived weapons in modern history. The basic construction was similar to that of the 1903 pistol—frame and slide—but the hammer was on the outside of the frame, where a glance could reveal whether or not the pistol was cocked. The barrel was held to the frame by a loose link, so that it could move rearward and, due to the link, downward. On top were two

lugs, which mated with two slots in the inner surface of the slide. With the pistol loaded, the lugs and slots engaged; on firing, the recoil force drove barrel and slide back, locked together for a short distance, taking up the time it took for the bullet to leave the barrel. Then, due to the link, the rear of the barrel moved downwards, so withdrawing the lugs from the slide. The barrel stopped moving, but the momentum that had been imparted to the slide made it continue rearward, extracting and ejecting the spent case, cocking the hammer, and then returning under spring power to load a fresh round. Once the cartridge was in the chamber, the slide, moving forward, pushed on the barrel, so lifting it back into engagement with the slide as it came to rest ready to fire again.

This, the "Browning swinging link" system of breech locking is another design that has been copied widely. The only change was to

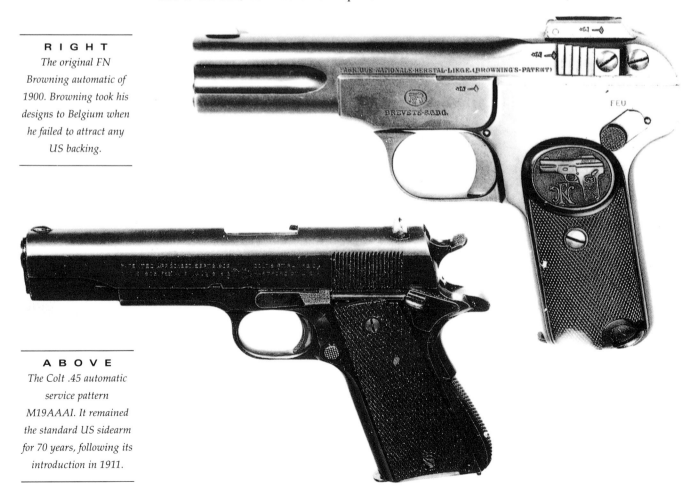

RIGHT
The original FN Browning automatic of 1900. Browning took his designs to Belgium when he failed to attract any US backing.

ABOVE
The Colt .45 automatic service pattern M19AAAI. It remained the standard US sidearm for 70 years, following its introduction in 1911.

alter the swinging link into a much simpler system; a lug of metal beneath the barrel has a shaped slot cut in it, which engages with a pin passing through the frame. As the barrel moves back, so the slot passes across the pin and its curved surface draws the barrel downward. The result is the same, but manufacture becomes slightly simpler. Another modification has been to do away with the upstanding lugs on the barrel and the slots in the slide and simply shape the rear end of the barrel to form the lock. The result is the same but manufacture is easier.

BROWNING HIGH POWER

The Browning Model 1935 in 9mm Luger, also known as the GP35 or High Power, was developed from locked breech designs Browning left when he died in 1926. The designs were patented by FN in 1927, and following its launch in 1935, the GP35 became the most popular military pistol of the noncommunist countries.

HECKLER & KOCH P7

A new modern design, the German Heckler & Koch P7 9mm self-loading pistol utilizes propellant gas to aid its operation. A 9mm Luger is too powerful a cartridge to be used with ease in a lightweight, straight blowback pistol. To reduce the pressure on the breech, the P7 uses a gas-retarded action, where some propellant gas is bled off from the barrel into a cylinder machined in the frame, into which the recoil spring guide fits. The gas pressure on firing pushes against the recoil spring guide, delaying the rearward movement of the slide. When the bullet leaves the barrel, the gas pressure in the cylinder drops and the slide can then recoil, now being controlled by recoil spring. The 7 also uses squeeze-cocking, where the pressure of the shooter's grip cocks the hammer/striker prior to firing. If the grip is released, the pistol decocks. This system eliminates the need for safety catches or a combined double and single action trigger mechanism.

GAS OPERATED PISTOLS

Gas operation makes self-loading pistols bulky and complex, as well as requiring a very powerful cartridge to generate enough gas to cycle the action. The Wildey pistol has made it to the market with two caliber options, both produced specifically for it, the .45 Winchester Magnum and the 9mm Winchester Magnum. The Wildey utilizes a rotating breech block as well as gas operation, a feature shared by the Israel Military Industries' Desert Eagle Pistol, which fires the .44 Magnum and .357 Magnum rimmed revolver cartridges. Both were designed with handgun hunting in mind, rather than for self-defence. AMT's Auto-mag II uses a gas assisted action with a rimfire .22 WMR caliber.

AUTOMATIC RIFLES

B Y THE early years of this century the automatic machine gun had come into use and inventors began contemplating how to make a rifle automatic in its action, so that a soldier could simply maintain his aim and keep pulling the trigger. Indeed, the Danish Navy had adopted an automatic rifle as early as the 1890s, though it failed to last and later became a light machine gun. Other designs were put forward, notably the Italian Cei-Rigotti of 1900 and the Mexican Mondragon of 1907, but they proved cumbersome and too complicated to withstand active service. It was not until 1932 that a major army adopted an automatic rifle as standard, when the US Army settled on the Garand.

The invention of John Garand, working at the Springfield Armory, this .30in rifle was gas-operated, tapping a small portion of the propellant gas from the barrel and using it to drive back a piston. This was linked to the bolt, so as to rotate and open it and then thrust it back against a spring. After the thrust died away, the spring forced the bolt and piston back, collecting a cartridge from the magazine and loading it, simultaneously cocking the firing mechanism. The magazine held eight rounds in a clip; after the last round had been fired, the bolt stayed open and the clip was ejected ready for reloading. Though somewhat heavier than the Springfield it replaced, the Garand was a robust and reliable weapon, which served the US Army well for over 30 years, though strictly it was a

"semiautomatic" rather than a true automatic weapon—it fired one shot and reloaded, waiting for the firer to pull the trigger for the next shot. Automatic fire could have been provided, but was not practical; firing such a powerful cartridge at high rates caused a hand-held weapon to become uncontrollable and simply waste ammunition.

The Soviets had discovered this already; in the 1920s they had adopted small numbers of the Federov automatic rifle, designed in 1916 around the Japanese 6.5mm rifle cartridge, large numbers of which had been captured by Russia during the Russo-Japanese War of 1904–1905. This low-powered round produced a weapon that was more controllable, but it proved somewhat fragile and, in the chaos of the revolution and its aftermath, the idea was abandoned. When the Americans put Garand into service, however, Soviet interest was rekindled and two designs, the Simonov of 1936 and the Tokarev of 1938, were produced. Both fired the full-power 7.62mm rifle cartridge and both proved to be too much of a handful and too fragile for general service, the Tokarev finally being used as a specialist sniping rifle.

The German Army also looked closely at the automatic rifle concept. Mauser had made experimental weapons during World War I, but none were acceptable. Though various inventors put up ideas in between the wars, it was not until 1940 that the Army finally put forward

B E L O W
The Soviet-designed AK-47 Kalashnikov, the most prolifically manufactured rifle in armaments' history. This example comes from China.

A B O V E
*The Colt M16A2 rifle
(model 701), standard US
Army issue.*

an official demand for such a weapon. The answer was the Walther G41, an odd weapon that used the muzzle blast to drive a cup forward to actuate the reloading mechanism. It was not a success and, being temperamental and badly balanced and production was soon stopped although the rifle continued in use until 1945.

A more significant development was the FG42, a special rifle developed for the German parachute forces. Like the G41, this used the standard 7.92mm rifle cartridge, a powerful round, but clever design made it almost controllable in automatic fire. As a single shot weapon, the bolt was closed and locked before firing; in the automatic mode, the bolt stayed open be-

tween bursts, allowing the barrel to cool. It was laid out in a straight line instead of having the traditionally dropped butt, so that the recoil went into the shoulder directly and had little tendency to lift the muzzle away from the target. The magazine fed from the side, metal and plastic were used in its manufacture, and the whole thing weighted less than ten pounds. Unfortunately, it was expensive and slow to manufacture; it was also a Luftwaffe rather than an Army weapon (the parachute troops came under the German Air Force), so it never went into army service and no more than 7,000 were made. More successful was the MP44, the ancestor of all the assault rifles which have proliferated ever since.

R I G H T
*A US infantryman on
exercise, armed with his
Colt M16A2 rifle, a
handy combat weapon.*

EXCEPT FOR a few short-lived experiments, the remaining armies of World War II went to war with slightly improved versions of the bolt-action rifles they had carried in 1914–1918, and it was not until the war was over that serious work began on replacing all these with automatic weapons. The first to go into service (though it was not known in the west for several years) was the Soviet Kalashnikov AK47, designed around a new 7.62mm short cartridge that probably owed something to the German assault rifle round. The Kalashnikov was simple and tough, could fire single shots or automatically at 600 rounds a minute, was gas-operated and used a 30-shot magazine. It is probably the most prolifically produced and distributed rifle in history, upwards of 40 million having been turned out in the past 40 years; production of the Kalashnikov and of its copies of it still goes on in many countries.

Britain was also impressed by the German short-case cartridge argument and developed a 7mm round and a rifle to go with it in the last 1940s. This was the EM2 (Enfield Model 2), a revolutionary design years ahead of its time. The layout of the rifle was what is known (for no very good reason) as a "bullpup," meaning that the actual breech is right at the butt end of the rifle, under the firer's ear. In a bullpup, with the breech against the end of the butt, the length of the breech and barrel is the length of the rifle, so that the same length of barrel can be accommodated inside shorter overall length.

The EM2 was approved for service as the Rifle No. 9 in 1951, but it was cancelled before production. At that time, the first stirrings of NATO standardization were in the air, and a common small arms round was among the first priorities. The Canadian and French armies were favorably disposed to the British 7mm round, but the Americans were implacably against it. Eventually, for the sake of NATO amity, Britain gave up its rifle and cartridge, adopting the American 7.62mm cartridge (which was simply the .30 bullet in a slightly shorter case) and the Belgian Fabrique National FAL rifle to go with it. The United States set about reworking the Garand to make it capable of automatic fire and gave it a 20-round box magazine, calling the result the 7.62mm M14

ABOVE
The SIG 550 Sniper rifle.

BELOW
The 7.62mm Galil semi-automatic, produced by Israel Military Industries.

ABOVE
The Walther WA 2000, complete with special Zeiss sight.

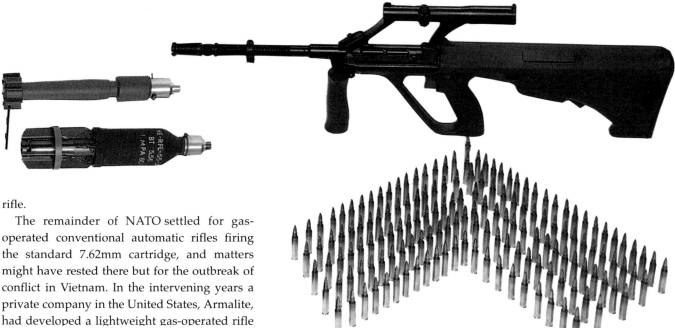

rifle.

The remainder of NATO settled for gas-operated conventional automatic rifles firing the standard 7.62mm cartridge, and matters might have rested there but for the outbreak of conflict in Vietnam. In the intervening years a private company in the United States, Armalite, had developed a lightweight gas-operated rifle firing a new .233in cartridge; this was largely due to the US Army searching for a new rifle that would give a higher "first round hit probability". Various solutions were tested, but the general consensus favored a light rifle firing a lighter bullet, so that aim disturbance due to recoil was minimal. This led Armalite to its .233 rifle, which it called the AR15. During the Vietnam war, the US Air Force purchased a number of these for use by airfield guards in Vietnam; they were seen by troops of the US Army, who opined that these rifles were just what was needed for jungle warfare. More were purchased, and, to cut a long story short, by the late 1960s the US Army had decided that the AR15, now known as the M16, would be their standard infantry rifle. This made nonsense of NATO standardization and also of their earlier refusal of the 7mm cartridge.

Faced with this, the rest of NATO had to think about its infantry armament. Most of the rifles adopted in the early 1950s were approaching the end of their economic lives, and by the 1980s would need replacement, so rifle designers began looking at the .223 (or, as it was now known, 5.56mm) cartridge. Although smaller than the standard 7.62mm caliber used hitherto, it had a high velocity and was amply lethal; the only drawback was that it had poor performance above 400 to 500 meters (440 to 550 yards) range. A number of designs appeared from private manufacturers, such as Beretta, Fabrique Nationale, and Heckler & Koch, but, rather than jump at any of them, NATO decided on a long and exhaustive test in the late 1970s, aimed at settling the question of what cartridge they would adopt as standard.

After four years of testing the result was the standardization of the 5.56mm cartridge, but with a heavier bullet. With this settled the armies could adopt new designs, and the British were among the first with their SA80 (for "Small Arm of the 80s"). However, perhaps the most astonishing of the European 5.56mm rifles was the Austrian AUG (for "Army Universal Gun") developed by Steyr-Mannlicher. This, too, was a bullpup design, introduced in the early 1980s, but was built in modular form so that various of its parts could be changed. The whole weapon is based on a strong plastic housing; the barrel can be quickly removed and exchanged for one of four different lengths, giving the options of submachine gun, carbine, rifle, or light machine gun. The receiver, inside which the bolt works, incorporates a carrying handle with built-in optical sight, but this can be changed for a receiver having merely a flat platform upon which any optical sight can be fitted.

The firing mechanism is of plastic construction and fits inside the butt.

A B O V E

The Steyr-Mannlicher AUG (AUG stands for "Army Universal Gun") is an extremely advanced 5.6mm design with interchangeable barrels, so the rifle can be swiftly converted.

NEW MATERIALS & MANUFACTURING TECHNIQUES

A T THE turn of the century, the transition from black powder to nitrocellulose propellants in handgun ammunition demanded stronger raw materials and better construction raw materials and better construction of the weapons themselves. Black powder was dirty and corrosive when burned, and generated low pressure in firearms' chambers and breeches. Even small quantitites of smokeless powders produced pressures approaching double those of the old gunpowders, and many early firearms exploded when they were inadvertently used with smokeless ammunition. For new handguns, better grades of steel and generally heavier construction were necessary to reap the improved performance benefits of the new propellants. Where brass had been used previously for frames, this was replaced with steel.

Wartime manufacture The escalating European military conflicts of the 20th century created a demand for firearms on a scale previously unseen. With little time to develop new methods of construction before World War I, the handguns used were produced in much the same was as they had been for the previous 20 years; the only use of rubber and early plastics was for grips, replacing wood. The principal cost saving in military weapons was in permitting wider manufacturing tolerances and cheapening the finish, using phosphate and crude blacking rather than the high polish and deep blacking used for commercial handguns.

Rearming for World War II, however, shortages of steel necessitated a dramatic redesign of fighting weapons. The submachine gun had been added to the world's arsenals, and, following Germany's lead with the MP38, these were cheaply made from pressed steel, plastics, and wire. The handgun was still regarded as a weapon of last resort, for close quarters defense. The United States issued the steel and wood M1 .30 carbine to its GIs as a manageable assault weapon, although it still continued to supply the hard kicking 1911A1 pistol to more seasoned soldiers who could control it. Other armies only issued handguns to officers, as defensive weapons for confined spaces such as in tanks or aircraft, or as special silenced versions for covert operations. Simple pressed

*Smith & Wesson's five
shot .38in Chiefs Special
was the first commercial
revolver to be made
entirely from stainless
steel giving it unrivaled
resistance to corrosion.*

steel pistols were dropped behind enemy lines for use by resistance organisations. As in World War I, the main savings with handguns were in finish rather than design and material.

Plating for protection The handgun was principally used as a personal defense weapon from the time it was invented, and as such was carried in pockets, holsters, or tucked into belts. The proximity of human sweat to a concealed weapon, or of exposure to the elements if carried in an external holster, caused rapid surface corrosion to handguns. Many 19th-century Western revolvers were available in a nickel-plated finish to improve the resistance of the steel frame and cylinders. This tradition was carried over into the 20th century, especially for "pocket pistols," small-framed pistols and revolvers of fairly small calibers which were frequently nickel, chrome or silver-plated. Hard

chroming, which toughens the surface of steel, has now become commonplace, especially on hunting and IPSC competition pistols.

Stainless steels The pressures and stresses involved in firearms precluded the use of any other material than carbon steel for the bulk of their construction for many years. Stainless steel would appear to be an ideal material—being an alloy of iron with up to 20 percent chromium and 12 percent nickel—which had been used in industry since World War I. It was not used for complete firearms, however, until 1965, when Smith & Wesson introduced the Model 60 Chief's Special, a small frame shot .38 revolver. This was partly due to the cost of the material and the difficulty of machining it, since tools used on stainless steels wear out up to five times faster than they do when used on mild or even high carbon steels. Another stumbling block was the problem of galling, where stainless steel parts rubbing against each other "pick up" particles from the other, leaving a rough surface. This caused semiautomatic pistols to jam unless carefully lubricated with

special oils. Stainless steels were also softer than carbon steel and would not hold the edge needed for trigger sears; they would also wear around pivot points, which resulted in revolvers requiring frequent gunsmithing to keep them in tune. It was found that by using different grades of stainless steel for rubbing parts, galling was reduced, and later developments in alloys improved the wear resistance considerably.

.44 Auto Mag One of the first wholly stainless self-loading pistols was the .44 Auto Mag launched in 1971 by Harry Sanford of Pasedena, California. Sanford used cut down .308 rifle cases to make the ammunition for the Auto Mag. Like many mold-breaking designs, it was not a commercial success in the conservative world of handguns, partly due to the lack of availability of ammunition.

Stainless steel is now a common handgun material, with Smith & Wesson, Colt, Ruger, and Walther all making versions of their revolvers or pistols in both stainless and carbon steels. Some of the new US firearms manufacturers, such as Detonics, Freedom Arms, AMT, and Randall, only use stainless for their weapons. The Israeli Desert Eagle pistol is now available with a stainless frame, as is the Colt Elite.

ABOVE
Small specialized manufacturers like Detonics only use high-grade stainless steel in the production of their self-loading pistols.

The use of stainless steel is appreciated by black powder shooters who delight in using the vintage propellant for target shooting, and hunting with old firearms and their replicas. The residue left by black powder on firing is highly corrosive, and many replicas are available in stainless steel versions.

Investment casting Modern investment or lost wax casting methods have improved the speed and quality of production, as well as reducing costs. Casting has been around since metals were first melted and poured into sand molds, but cast parts were frequently brittle and porous, unsuitable for lightweight load- or pressure-bearing parts. For these components, the traditional method of manufacture was to take a big lump of high-quality steel and machine off anything that did not look like a gun.

Cost saving in handgun production has become as critical as quality; military orders for handguns are based on price and volume, and civilian sales are dropping worldwide due to pressure from domestic anti-gun lobby groups. Computer-controlled lathes and mills can be used for machining, but cheaper ways of production are still needed and investment casting has produced the biggest breakthrough. Lost wax or investment casting starts from an injection-molded was "positive" form of the final product. This is coated with a liquid ceramic which is first dried then baked. The wax melts, leaving a perfect "negative" mold into which the molten metal is injected. When set, the ceramic mold is broken off leaving a high quality casting which needs little machining and can be made in a complex shape. The minimal machining required makes the technique most suitable for hard-to-work stainless steels, or any part which would normally need extensive finishing.

Ruger P85 A contemporary pioneer in handgun production technology is Bill Ruger of Sturm Ruger, a US company established in New England. Now established as a manufacturer of

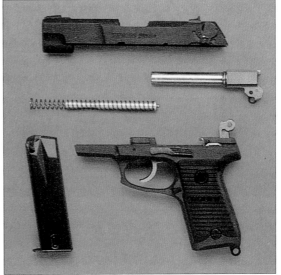

Ruger's latest pistol, the
9mm P85, is almost
entirely cast,
substantially reducing
the manufacturing cost.

RUGER P-85

single action Colt 1911 has more than 60 parts, a modern double action revolver, over 70.) The pistol is almost entirely cast—investment-cast chrome-moly steel slide, investment-cast aluminum alloy frame, and the majority of the stainless steel internal parts are investment cast, too. The grips are injection-molded "Xenoy" plastic, and the pistol has a barrel and chamber made from two pieces screwed together.

Aluminum alloys The Ruger P85 uses an aluminium alloy frame for lightness. Aluminum is a soft, ductile metal, with similar galling problems to stainless steel when used for rubbing parts. The tensile strength of early alloys was also low, so it could not be used for stressed parts. However, since many handguns are carried a lot and shot very little, some stronger aluminum alloys have been used in the past for pistol and revolver frames. Alloy frames have been particularly popular in those pistols carried day in and day out by bodyguards, such as the Colt Commander 9mm pistol, or the lightweight Charter Arms .38 and .44 revolvers. The latest aluminum alloys claim to have a tensile strength far higher than that of steel, and use in frames is becoming common. The impact resistance of aluminum is not yet good enough for slides and heavily stressed barrels; Colt's experiment with lightweight aluminum revolver cylinders for air crew during the Korean War ended in 1951 when the idea was rejected by US Air Force for .38 revolvers, and by the public for .32 and .22 revolvers in 1955. The American Derringer Corporation has made one of its vast range of derringers in .38 Spl with a stainless steel frame and aluminum barrels. Smith & Wesson's new lightweight trail pistol, the Model 422, has a high tensile alloy frame and barrel shroud, with pressed steel trigger and action components to produce one of the lowest price, quality, .22 semiautomatics available.

Exotic alloys Other exotic alloys have not been so popular. High tensile manganese bronze has been used in only two handguns, the Century Arms Model 100 Single Action revolver and the Golden Bison Super 6. Beryllium copper has been used for the firing pins in Charter Arms re-

high quality, low priced and rugged handguns making extensive use of investment castings, Ruger has recently launched his first pistol in 9mm Luger, the P85. The operating concepts of the double action pistol are not new, still relying on Browning's turn of the century swinging-link, locked-breech principles. The method of manufacture is fully up to date and Ruger has built a factory in Prescott, Arizona, US, to assemble the new pistol which has been designed with only 50 parts in it. (The "simple"

RIGHT
The Smith & Wesson Model 686. .357 Magnum is one of the most popular stainless steel revolvers available today.

DIRECT
Alloy frames are now common in modern service pistols. Models from the Beretta 92 series in 9mm Luger have been adopted for military and police use in the US and France.

volvers, and is being investigated for use in pistol frames by Para Ordnance in Canada. Titanium is very strong and extremely light in alloys, but is also extremely expensive. Göncz of California uses titanium to line the barrels of their High Tech pistols and this is claimed to reduce barrel wear significantly. Göncz also uses very modern coatings to prevent wear in other parts of its pistols, which can also be silenced and used as grenade launchers.

Plastic pistols Attention is now turning to plastics, carbon fibers and ceramics for new handgun designs. Although rubber, and later plastics, have been used for handgun grips since the 1850s, it took an Austrian engineer who had never designed a pistol before to make extensive structural use of plastics in the Glock 17 pistol. The frame, trigger, and magazines of the Glock are all plastic, which led to media scares worldwide that the Libyans would soon be supplying them to terrorists and hijackers since they would not be detectable at airports by metal detectors or X-ray machines. In fact, the Glock still has a steel slide and barrel which contains more metal than some conventional lightweight pocket pistols, and both the Glock and its metal-cased, metal-primed, and metal-bulleted 9mm ammunition are readily detectable by existing security devices.

Hämmerli's Model 280 .22 target pistol is

made with carbon fiber for much of its frame, and indicates the direction target pistol manufacture is heading in. Small bore and target pistols for Olympic and international events are shielded from service constraints of concealability, portability, and reliability under field conditions, and while some of their developments have not been adopted by mainstream manufacturers, the research can often be refined for service use.

Ceramics Ceramics are usually thought of as brittle, temperature-resistant compounds, more suited to high-tech casting or electronics than handguns. But in the 1980s there were reports that the Eastern Bloc has developed an all plastic gun which fires a ceramic bullet from a plastic case, in an attempt to defeat security devices.

Handgun materials today The popular revolvers of today, such as the Smith & Wesson Model 686, are made from stainless steel, and the trend for self-loading pistols is for strong alloy frames and carbon steel slides. The high capacity Beretta 92F in 9mm Luger has just such a construction and it has been adopted as the new service pistol in both the United States and France. Single shot pistols are made with investment-cast frames, but their emphasis is on strength rather than cost reduction.

From Powder Shot to Percussion

FIREARMS DESIGNS are many and diverse. However, they all share one common feature, in that they burn a propellant in a closed chamber. This burning is exceedingly rapid and generates large quantities of hot gas. The gas pressure is contained behind a projectile, usually a bullet, which blocks the only way out of the chamber. When the pressure generated by the burning propellant is sufficiently high, the bullet is driven out of the chamber and down the gun's barrel.

THE BEGINNING

The origins of black powder or gunpowder are far from clear. The first written record in the West is in an anagram concealed in a scientific treatise written by Roger Bacon in 1242. The first open record is in another Bacon treatise, written in 1266, in which he refers to "the powder, known in divers places, composed of saltpeter, charcoal and sulfur." This implies that it was generally known by that time, but the context suggests that it was simply a scientific oddity, something to startle and amaze people, which had no specific use. It was not until the

gun was developed that the powder was found to have a practical application. But Bacon never revealed the origin of the powder and over the years there have been several other claimants to its invention. Exhaustive research has not produced any definite result, but it is now generally accepted that it was probably developed by the Arabs and then found its way into Europe. The frequently stated belief that it originated in China seems to have little foundation.

The formula given by Bacon in his 1242 manuscript called for 41.2 percent saltpeter, 29.3 percent sulfur and 29.5 percent charcoal; it is doubtful if the materials of the day were very pure, and this, together with the stated proportions, leads to the conclusion that the powder was relatively weak. It was made by grinding the individual ingredients in a dry state, and then mixing them by hand to produce a fine powder. When the powder was poured into a gun, it settled into a dense body. This made ignition difficult as the flame could not penetrate the fine mass very quickly. It led to erratic action and inconsistent performance.

This weakness, however, was a blessing in

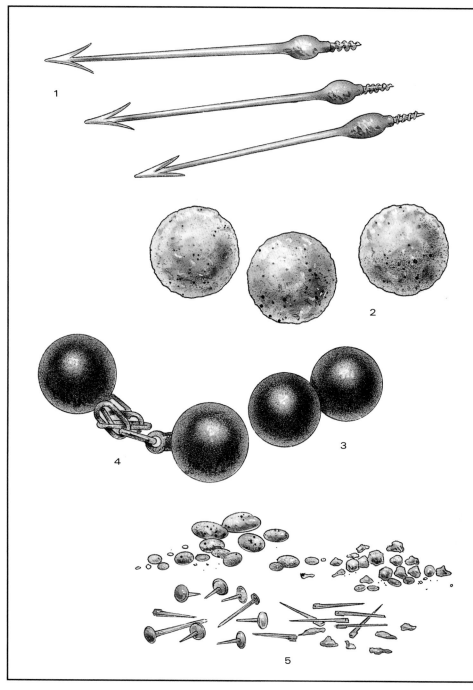

1 The very first cannon fired arrows, simply because the arrow was the most familiar projectile. The shaft had to be found with rags to make it fit the gun barrel.

2 Later came stone shot, since stone was freely available, easily worked into shape, and did not strain the gun.

3 Stronger guns allowed the use of metal shot. While this meant casting and more expense, spent shot could sometimes be retrieved and reused.

4 Chaining two shot together was an effective antipersonnel weapon.

5 Langridge was the term used to describe the collection of scrap metal, horseshoe nails, gravel, and anything else calculated to wound, loaded into the gun.

disguise as the early guns could not have withstood a more effective and powerful powder. Stone shot was commonly used because it weighed less than an equivalent iron ball, so that when the powder was ignited the stone shot moved off quickly and prevented a build-up of high pressure behind it. Firing an iron ball of large caliber would probably have burst the gun before the shot left the muzzle.

The earliest guns used arrows. The arrow was a missile that was accepted and understood, and by binding the shaft with leather until it fitted into the gun bore, it could be launched with some degree of accuracy. But arrows of a size and strength to withstand firing were difficult to make and expensive, and therefore the iron ball was developed. However, once the drawbacks outlined above made themselves known, the stone ball was widely adopted instead. It was cheap and effective; it could batter down light structures; it could kill and injure unprotected men, and if it struck a hard surface it would shatter, showering the area with dangerous fragments.

Gunpowder The first gunpowder, known as "serpentine powder," had another defect. When it was carried in barrels and subjected to jolting, the heavy saltpeter and sulfur tended to settle to the bottom of the barrel, leaving the lighter

charcoal on top, so that the gunner had to remix the powder before he could use it. The first ammunition improvement came in the early 15th century and is believed to have originated in France. This was the manufacture of "corned powder" in which the three ingredients were first ground, and then well wetted and mixed together. The resulting "cake" was dried and broken up before being passed through a sieve to obtain a consistent size of grains. When these were loaded into the gun, they did not pack so tightly as serpentine powder and thus the ignition flame could pass between them and ignite the whole charge almost instantaneously. The result was that for a given weight, corned powder was about three times as powerful as serpentine. It was also less susceptible to damp, unaffected by shaking or jolting, and was easier to handle, and it left less residue after firing. The only drawback was that it was too powerful for the built-up guns of the period, and therefore its adoption had to wait until cast guns became a possibility.

With cast guns and corned powder the iron ball came back into favor as the standard projectile. Iron was relatively cheap and a simple mold allowed balls to be cast very easily, whereas stone balls had to be laboriously hand-shaped. The loss of the shattering effect of stone on impact was more than balanced by the greater force which the improved powder, stronger guns, and iron balls could deliver.

The only real drawback to the ball was its limited effect against personnel: fired into a mass of men it would only damage those on its trajectory, leaving their companions to either side unharmed. To compensate for this many ingenious arrangements of balls linked with chains or iron bars were invented, so that they would swing in flight and thus carve a wider path of destruction.

No matter how magnificent a firearm may be, it is useless if there is no ammunition. One of the greatest drawbacks to almost every early form of firearm was the fact that after the shot had been fired the weapon was useful only as a bludgeon. At best, loading was a slow business, and the use of a powder flask, priming powder and a bullet involved a considerable number of movements. Attempts to speed up loading were made from the earliest days, and one of the first was a wooden or horn container that held just one charge of powder. Twelve were suspended from a belt or bandoleer, worn over one shoulder and across the chest.

For the military speed of reloading could be vital, and paper cartridges were developed. A strip of thick paper was rolled around a wooden former to make a tube, and one end was closed by twisting the paper. A charge of powder was poured in, a ball placed on top, and the other end closed by another twist. Each soldier carried a supply of these paper cartridges in some form of pouch. The cartridges were a little vulnerable, so they were sometimes carried in wooden blocks drilled with holes to accommodate each cartridge. To load his musket or pistol the soldier bit off one twisted end, poured a pinch of powder into the pan and then tipped the rest down the barrel, adding the paper at the end to serve as a wad. He then rammed down the bullet using the ramrod. Similar cartridges were made for the percussion revolvers, but these often had a small tag made of material that could be pulled to split open the paper and release the powder.

A few handguns were produced that did not need the paper to be torn, for the cartridge contained not only the powder but also enclosed a small capsule of percussive compound. The cartridge was loaded into the breech of the gun and the detonation was achieved by a long, thin needle, which was punched forward to puncture the paper, hit the percussive pellet, and so fire the charge. Their success was limited and few examples of the cartridges have survived.

With the advent of the percussion system there arose the need to fit small caps onto small nipples, and in bad weather or with cold fingers this was an irksome task. To speed up and simplify matters cap dispensers were designed. These are commonly of two types—either a flat disk or a long, rectangular bar. Both incorporate a spring, which is compressed as it is loaded with caps, and the open end has a spring that retains the last cap over an opening. To cap a chamber or the breech of a rifle, the exposed cap is pressed on the nipple and the dispenser pulled clear. The retaining spring allows the next cap to move along and then grips it ready for the next loading.

From the earliest times there were numerous attempts to overcome the serious limitation of

The Lilliput, which was produced in Germany in the late 1920s, is so small that it is really more of a model than a real weapon. Its size alone makes it something of a collector's piece, and examples are not common. The Kolibri, which was made in Austria, is even smaller at only 3mm caliber. The tiny center-fire cartridges are also keenly collected.

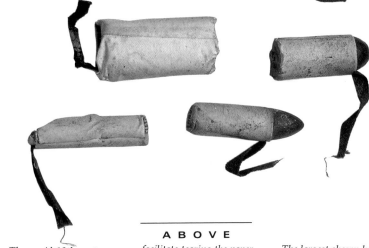

having only a single shot, and the most popular and simple was the double-barreled weapon. Some had the barrels mounted side by side and others one on top of the other. The principle was extended to three- and four-barreled weapons, but even this system was comparatively slow because of the steps that were necessary before each shot could be fired.

Another solution was the superimposed load technique. The barrel was made with two touchholes, and the first charge of powder and ball was poured down the barrel so that it was adjacent to the rear touchhole. A substantial wad was then located in front of the bullet and the second charge poured down, which was then next to the front touchhole. By various ingenious arrangements of the ignition system the front charge was fired first, followed by the rear charge, a system that gave a reasonably rapid two-shot capability. The loading and sequence of firing was obviously vital, and should the rear charge be fired first or both shots fired together there was likely to be a nasty accident.

Matchlock, wheel-lock, and flintlock revolvers were only a limited success, for the ignition system was mechanically difficult and awkward to design. It was the advent of the percussion system and, ultimately, the percussion cap that opened the door to a cure for the problem. The cap first made possible pepperbox revolvers and then, in the middle of the 19th century, the percussion revolver. These new weapons gave a firepower of a usual six

A B O V E

These mid-19th-century paper cartridges were manufactured by Eley Brothers, the famous London ammunition firm. The tape projecting from the tip of each was to *facilitate tearing the paper to release the gunpowder. The smaller cartridges were for the .31in Pocket Colt percussion revolver, and others were made for the Adams .45in revolver.* *The largest shown here is a 15 gauge, with a caliber of .68in. The fragility of these cartridges made it unlikely that they will survive.*

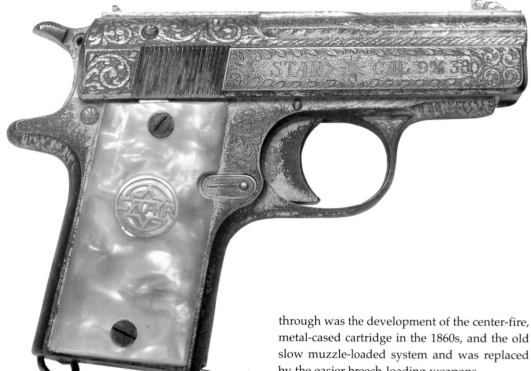

shots and with some rather cumbersome pinfire revolvers as many as 30 or more shots. Nevertheless, despite the great advance in weapon technology, the percussion revolver and, to a much lesser degree, the pinfire revolver were still rather slow in loading. The final break-

through was the development of the center-fire, metal-cased cartridge in the 1860s, and the old slow muzzle-loaded system and was replaced by the easier breech-loading weapons.

Breech-loading was not new—attempts had been made from the earliest days of firearms to use it. Early cannon were mostly breech-loading, but these and later systems all suffered from one great problem—leakage of gas. In order to load at the breech some means of access was obviously necessary, but to achieve this there had to be some sort of opening. It was easy enough to devise this, but the problem was to make certain that when the charge was ignited the breech was sealed to ensure that all the gases generated expanded along the barrel to propel the missile with maximum force. It was also important to prevent leakage to protect the operator from the unpleasant effects of flame and smoke that were blown out through gaps around the breech.

As early as 1812 the Swiss inventor Johannes Pauly had designed a center-fire cartridge with a brass base and a cardboard body just like the modern shotgun cartridge. Pauly's guns had drop-down barrels, and the cartridge was loaded into the breech in exactly the same way as modern shotguns. Despite its obvious advantages the system was not adopted and faded away, and specimens of the Pauly cartridge are rare.

METALLIC CARTRIDGES

ODERN HANDGUN ammunition started life with the .22in Short rimfire cartridge developed by Smith & Wesson in their Model No. 1 First Issue Revolver—the first American-made handgun to use the metallic cartridge-type which is still with us today. The rimfire round was far safer and more reliable in revolvers than both the percussion cap-and-ball and the Lefaucheux pinfire cartridge, designed by Houiller in 1836, which had become popular in Europe.

Rimfire ignition uses a ring of priming compound in the folded hollow rim of the case which ignites when crushed by a blow to the rim, in turn starting combustion of the main propellant charge. The idea started from a French patent of 1831 in which priming compound covered the whole of the inside of the cartridge head. Smith & Wesson's rimfire round was developed from the Flobert BB cap of 1845, a very low-powered round used for short-range indoor target practice.

Rimfire cartridges themselves had limitations. The first ones made were low in power, with a caliber of only .22in (5.56mm). The problem lay in the rimfire system itself. The rim of the cartridge had to be weak so that the priming compound could feel the impact of the hammer and ignite the powder charge. Making the cartridge larger was an obvious way to increase the power, but simply using a bigger case and bullet with more powder was not easy. The rim of the case still needed to be thin enough to allow ignition, but strong enough to contain the higher pressures needed to overcome the inertia of a heavy bullet.

One of the most powerful and effective rimfire cartridges made was the .56–56 Spencer. It fired a 350 grain (22.7 g) bullet at 1200 fps (366 mps) with a charge of 45 grains (2.9 g) of black powder. The .56–56 Spencer was the first of its big bore rimfire cartridges, which included the calibers .56–52, .56–50, and .56–46. The cartridge was designed for use in the Spencer rifle, which was patented in 1860. Spencer rifles first appeared during the Civil War in 1862, and were later credited with having given the Union armies a vital firepower advantage prior to their victory at Gettysburg.

Another rimfire cartridge that acquired a

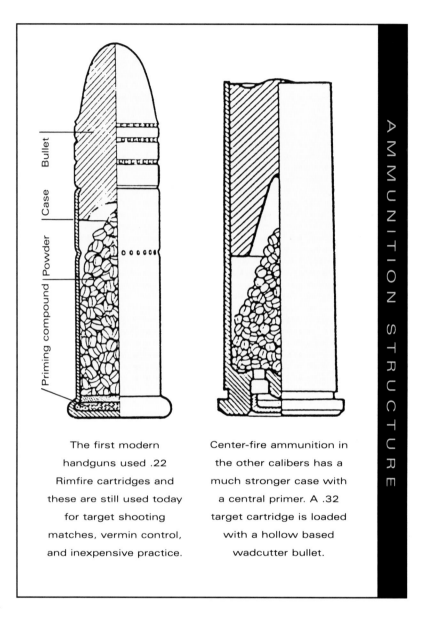

The first modern handguns used .22 Rimfire cartridges and these are still used today for target shooting matches, vermin control, and inexpensive practice.

Center-fire ammunition in the other calibers has a much stronger case with a central primer. A .32 target cartridge is loaded with a hollow based wadcutter bullet.

AMMUNITION STRUCTURE

well-deserved reputation was .44 Henry. The 15-shot Henry repeater of 1860 was the forerunner of the famous Winchester lever action rifle. It was not as powerful as the .56–56 Spencer, firing a 200 grain (13 g) bullet at 1,125 fps (3,443 mps). However, it could be used in revolvers, giving frontiersmen the opportunity to have a high-capacity rifle and 6-shot revolver which utilized the same ammunition.

Today rimfire ammunition is only produced in .22 caliber for rifled arms. Its principal uses are for pest control and target shooting.

The first revolver rounds were used in hand-

Ammunition for today's handguns comes in all calibers and types from .22 RF Short up to .454 Casull. Just part of the range is illustrated here with a Smith & Wesson Model 52 pistol. The Model 52 uses a .38 Special cartridge loaded with a flush flat nosed wadcutter bullet.

guns with parallel bored cylinders; this meant that the bullet and its cartridge case had to be of the same diameter as the cylinder, which in turn was the same bore as the barrel. Bullets of this type, known as "heeled" or "externally lubricated," are held in the case with a small recessed crimp at the base, leaving the bulk of the bullet and its lubricant coating exposed; this design is perpetuated today in the four .22 rimfire cartridges. By the time the 1873 Colt Peacemaker came on the scene, cartridges had been refined to contain the bullet in an oversized case which enclosed the bullet's grease grooves and the bearing surface, which bites into the barrel's

A B O V E

One of the most powerful cap-and-ball revolvers ever made was the 1847 Walker Colt. Only 1,100 originals were produced, but many working replicas like the Italian Uberti are still made in Europe. The muzzle loading cap-and-ball revolver does not use cartridges; black powder propellant is poured in the chambers and a round ball or conical bullet is rammed on top. Ignition is provided by the percussion cap on the nipple at the closed end of the chamber, which blases a flame into the chamber when hit by the hammer.

rifling. Smith & Wesson dropped the heeled .44 American cartridge in favor of .44 Russian, which eventually grew into the .44 cartridges available today. The chambers of revolvers were by this time stepped to accommodate the over-sized case, tapering down to ensure a good gas seal on the bullet as it left the case on firing. The cases retained a solid rim, which prevented the cartridge sliding forward into the chamber, and provided a headspace joint. The bullets were still made of lead and without metal jackets, since the low velocities of handgun ammunition—600–900 ft (183–274m) per second—did not cause significant lead fouling in the barrel.

In Britain the patent taken out by Colonel Edward Boxer in January 1866 changed the military cartridge for the British Army. The metal case, fashioned from thin brass sheet, was rolled around a metal former and then fitted to a base containing the primer. As a shot was fired the metal case expanded, effectively sealing the breech. The Boxer cartridge was primarily for rifles, but a .577in cartridge was produced for the Webley revolver. A .442in Boxer cartridge was also produced for the Royal Irish Constabulary revolver made by Webley in 1868. In the same year the converted Adams percussion revolver was officially adopted as the standard revolver for the British Army, and its .455in cartridge was a form of Boxer with a brass body and iron cup with the primer. It held 13 grains of black powder and a lead bullet with a hollow base, which was intended to concentrate the gases propelling it from the barrel.

The last step toward the current handgun cartridge was the introduction of a drawn brass case in place of the brass foil one, which tended to become separated from the base and jam the weapon. Because the handgun cartridge was much shorter than that of the rifle, it was easier and cheaper to produce a drawn brass case.

In 1873 a whole range of metal-cased cartridges was tested at the Frankford Arsenal, Philadelphia, and the end result was the development of an almost universal type of cartridge with a drawn brass case and a lead bullet. The only real difference between most US and British cartridges lay in the fitting of the cap. While the vast majority of British cases

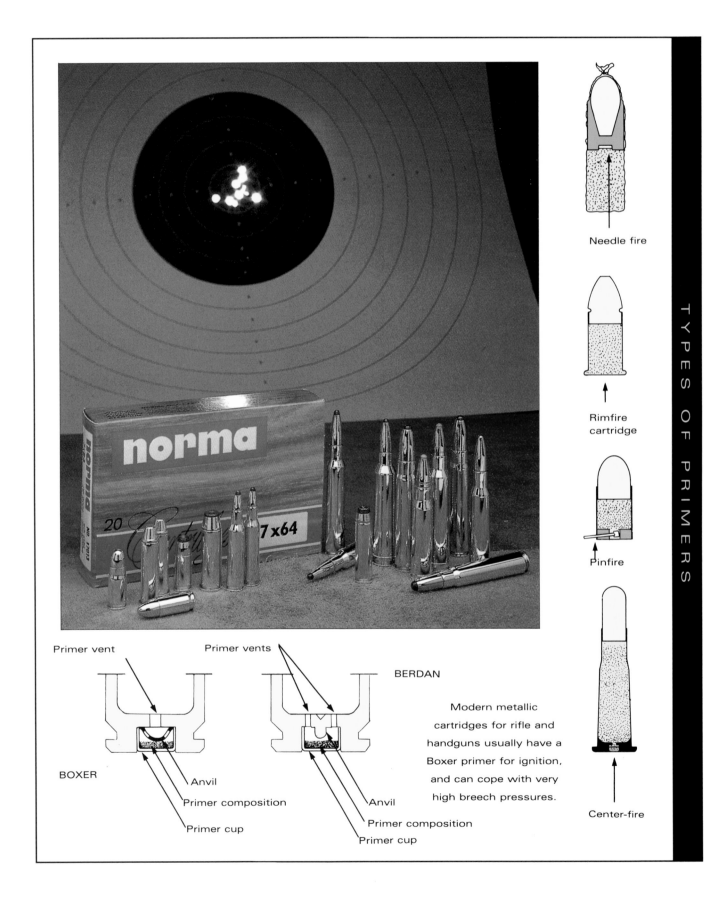

Primer vent

Primer vents

BERDAN

BOXER

Anvil

Primer composition

Primer cup

Anvil

Primer composition

Primer cup

Modern metallic cartridges for rifle and handguns usually have a Boxer primer for ignition, and can cope with very high breech pressures.

Needle fire

Rimfire cartridge

Pinfire

Center-fire

TYPES OF PRIMERS

L E F T
These metallic cartridges were made during the mid- and late-19th century. Two of them are pinfire: one, a 10mm caliber, has a card body and the other, a 9mm caliber, has a copper case. The small rimfire cartridge is approximately .38in caliber. The large cartridge is a center-fire .450in Kynoch cartridge, which was the round of the British Army officer's revolver. The tin of percussion caps, which were manufactured by Eley Brothers, would have come from a cased Colt Navy or Pocket revolver.

A B O V E
Black powder (left) gave way to to the smokeless propellant cordite (center left) at the turn of the century. Cordite itself has now been superseded by tubular and flake nitro-cellulose/nitroglycerine smokeless propellants (center right and right), and by ball powders (not shown).

used the Boxer system, many US metal-cased cartridges used a Berdan primer. Externally there is no apparent difference, but internally the Boxer cartridge has one central hole through the base leading to the cap, while the Berdan cartridge uses two small holes and a slightly different style of fitting.

The development of the breech-loading system led to a growth of interest in shooting. Sport, law enforcement, military, hunting, and self-defense interests all felt that they needed a special type of gun and, as often as not, a special cartridge. Expense was on consideration, but range and the ability to stop a charging animal or criminal were all factors that encouraged manufacturers to produce numerous cartridges. While the basic shape of the cartridges was similar, the sizes were very varied.

The method of describing cartridges became complex and it is still so today, with no generally accepted universal practice. In general, the diameter or caliber of the bullet is expressed in inches—.45in, .38in, or .22in, for example. In Europe, on the other hand, measurements are in millimeters, 9mm being the most common. However, some cartridges also have a second figure, and this may refer to the case length or to the powder charge. A black powder cartridge described as a .45–60 would mean that the bullet was .45in caliber and the black powder charge was 60 grains. Some cartridges are described with caliber and the name of the weapon for which it was made—9mm Steyr, for instance.

Caliber is a matter of choice, but in general indoor target shooters favor the .22in cartridge, for it is cheap and there is little recoil, making it easy to shoot a large number of rounds without discomfort. Since most indoor small bore target shooting is done at no more than 25 yards (23m), the powder charge and bullet need by only small. The .22in cartridge is also popular for small game shooting. There are two sizes of this popular caliber, .22in LR (long rifle) and .22in Short. Despite its name, the .22 LR is a popular pistol and revolver round, while .22in Short is preferred for rapid fire because the slide has a shorter distance to travel when extracting the case and the gun can then fire fractionally faster.

The developments of self-loading pistols in the 1890s followed the introduction of high-pressure smokeless propellants. Self-loaders worked best with rimless pistol rounds which were parallel-sided or bottle-necked, with a recessed rim or extractor groove for an extractor to grip during firing and cycling. Metallic jackets for the bullets were necessary to prevent lead build-up in the barrel. The Hague Convention for the rules of war effectively outlawed the use of exposed lead in service ammunition, even in those of low velocity, and a metal jacket of copper or steel became commonplace in military handgun ammunition. By the beginning of World War I the principal Western repeating pistol and revolver calibers had been established, and most subsequent "new" calibers were just lengthened and strengthened versions of the same thing. The world's two most popular handgun calibers today, 9mm Luger for pistols and .38in Smith & Wesson Special for revolvers, were both launched in 1902. Only in the second half of this century have any significantly new calibers been developed.

BELOW
This fine quality weapon is a Hammerli International .22in target pistol. The long barrel helps to increase accuracy, and the wooden grips are contoured for a firm, comfortable hold. Top-class shooters often have the butt grips specially molded to fit their hand exactly.

LEFT
A collector's box of rare 7.65mm Mauser ammunition. This would be welcome to a collector as it is complete and unopened.

BOLT-ACTION BALLISTICS

THE METALLIC cartridge case also brought out the potential of the bolt action rifle, which eventually became the world's most popular manually operated breech-loader. The Basic bolt action was first produced in Germany by Johann Nikolaus Dreyse who began work on a new rifle action and system of ignition in 1827. The Dreyse needle-fire rifle was adopted by the Prussian Army in 1840, and while the needle-fire cartridge has been confined to history, the breech-loading system the rifle used is the basis of all modern bolt actions.

Mauser 1898 By 1898 Mauser in Germany had refined the bolt action to the point where it has remained in used throughout the 20th century, albeit with a few minor changes. Mauser-type actions are used by virtually all the modern manufacturers of bolt action rifles. The heart of the '98 design is the bolt itself, which has two or more locking lugs on the bolt face and a third one at the back of the bolt. The bolt is essentially a long steel rod with a hole in the middle for the striker and its spring, a sprung extractor claw to remove the spent case, and an angled operating lever at the rear. The lugs engage in matching

A B O V E

Mauser's 1898 type rifle bolt (left) set the standard for others to follow. The .303 No. 4 rifle bolt has lugs at the rear rather than at the front on the Mauser. The Tikka bolt has both for extra strength.

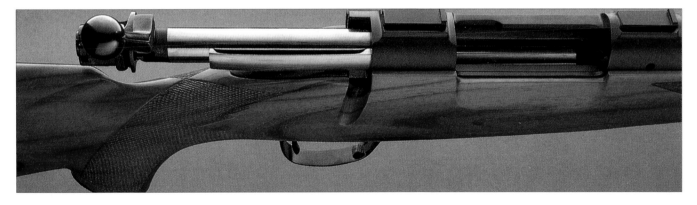

A B O V E

Mauser-derived bolt actions are now used almost universally by manufacturers of powerful bolt-action rifles, top: Kimber, below: Beretta.

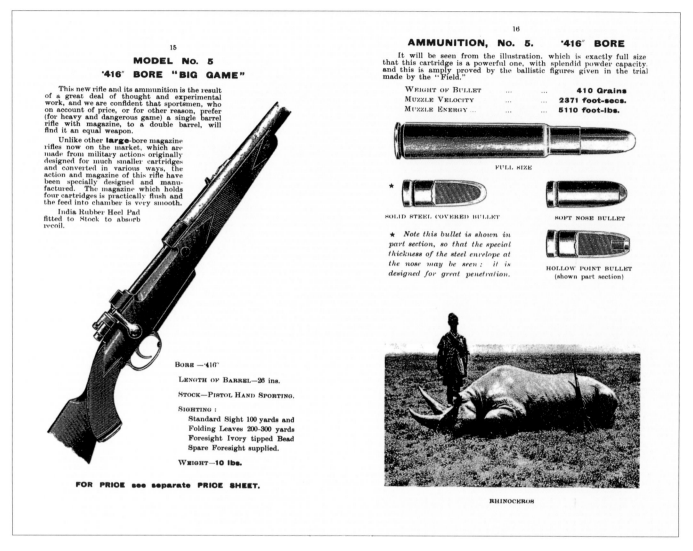

15

MODEL No. 5
'416" BORE "BIG GAME"

This new rifle and its ammunition is the result of a great deal of thought and experimental work, and we are confident that sportsmen, who on account of price, or for other reason, prefer (for heavy and dangerous game) a single barrel rifle with magazine, to a double barrel, will find it an equal weapon.

Unlike other **large**-bore magazine rifles now on the market, which are made from military actions originally designed for much smaller cartridges and converted in various ways, the action and magazine of this rifle have been specially designed and manufactured. The magazine which holds four cartridges is practically flush and the feed into chamber is very smooth.

India Rubber Heel Pad fitted to Stock to absorb recoil.

BORE —'416"

LENGTH OF BARREL—26 ins.

STOCK—PISTOL HAND SPORTING.

SIGHTING :
Standard Sight 100 yards and Folding Leaves 200-300 yards Foresight Ivory tipped Bead Spare Foresight supplied.

WEIGHT—10 lbs.

FOR PRICE see separate PRICE SHEET.

16

AMMUNITION, No. 5.   '416" BORE

It will be seen from the illustration, which is exactly full size that this cartridge is a powerful one, with splendid powder capacity, and this is amply proved by the ballistic figures given in the trial made by the "Field."

WEIGHT OF BULLET	...	...	**410 Grains**
MUZZLE VELOCITY	...	...	**2371 foot-secs.**
MUZZLE ENERGY ...	...	...	**5110 foot-lbs.**

FULL SIZE

SOLID STEEL COVERED BULLET

SOFT NOSE BULLET

★ *Note this bullet is shown in part section, so that the special thickness of the steel envelope at the nose may be seen: it is designed for great penetration.*

HOLLOW POINT BULLET
(shown part section)

RHINOCEROS

lugs in the receiver as the bolt is turned with the operating lever. This mechanically locks together the two parts making a very strong breech that can cope with very high pressures. A slightly different locking arrangement is used in the Austrian Steyr-Mannlicher action which locks at the rear of the bolt with six lugs.

Within the bolt is a spring-loaded firing pin or striker. The striker is cocked as the breech is unlocked by the action of a cam at the rear of the bolt. Pulling the trigger when the action is closed releases the striker, which hits the primer and ignites the cartridge. To reload, the bolt is worked upward and then backward, unlocking the breech cocking the striker and extracting the spent cartridge. The empty case is thrown out of the breech at rear of the bolt's travel when it hits

an ejector stub. As the bolt is worked forward it picks up a fresh cartridge and pushes it into the chamber ready for the next shot. High rates of fire can be achieved with bolt action rifles, but not quite the rapidity that can be reached with lever actions. The bolt action rifle was the standard service arm of the foot soldier in both World Wars and other lesser conflicts immediately before the turn of the century.

The power that can be generated in a bolt action rifle is very high indeed and original military and commercial Mauser 98 actions are the basis of the high-powered rifles made for use in Africa by Rigby, Holland & Holland, and Westley Richards in the UK. These are made for big game hunting and all the manufacturers have designed their own cartridges.

A B O V E
Rigby introduced the .416 Rigby cartridge for their rifles in 1911. By the time their 1924 catalogue was produced if had established a reputation as an accurate and powerful big-game round.

.375 Holland & Holland Introduced in 1912, Holland & Holland's .375 Belted Rimless Magnum is regarded as one of the most effective medium-bore African cartridges. Holland & Holland still produces bolt action rifles on Magnum Mauser actions chambered for .375 H&H Magnum, as do a host of other manufacturers. The belted case added strength to the web of the cartridge, and many other high-performance proprietary and wildcat cartridges have been based on the .375 H&H case. (See pages 151–153.) Most ammunition manufacturers produce a .375 H&H load, with a 270 or 300 grain (17.5/19.4 g) bullet. The lighter bullet has slightly more velocity and muzzle energy, 2740 fps (835 mps) and 4500 ft lb (6,098 joules).

A .30 caliber belted rimless cartridge was introduced by Holland & Holland in 1930 and it became renowned as a fine long range round when the 1000 yard Wimbledon Cup match was won with it in 1935. The velocity and energy of .300 H&H Magnum just exceeds that of .30–06 Springfield.

.416 Rigby John Rigby & Co introduced the .416 Rigby cartridge in 1911 for its Mauser Magnum action rifle, and like Holland & Holland it still produces rifles chambered for it today. Since original commercial square bridge Mauser actions are becoming scarce and expensive, Rigby will build a .416 rifle on a choice of actions at the customer's request, including those of Dakota and Ruger from the United States, the Heym from Germany, Dumoulin from Belgium, and BRNO from the Czech Republic. The .416 Rigby can be used for all big game and it fires a 410 grain (26.6 g) bullet to 2371 fps (723 mps) for an energy of 5,100 ft lb (6,911 joules). Of the American rifle manufacturers, Ruger's Model

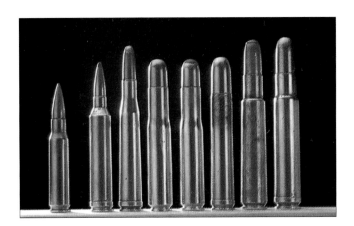

77 Magnum is the only one chambered for just .375 H&H and .416 Rigby.

.425 Westley Richards Magnum The performance of the .416 Rigby is slightly superior to that of .425 Westley Richards, which was first sold in 1909 with a 410 grain (26.6 g) bullet traveling at 2350 fps (716 mps) giving an energy of 5,030 ft lb (6,931 joules)—an academic distinction to the animal on the receiving end. The .425 Westley Richards has a shorter cartridge case than .416 Rigby and does not require the long Magnum action. The first cartridges had a rebated rim to allow the use of a standard Mauser bolt face. There is now an "improved" version available with a standard rimless case but it does not have any better ballistics than the original.

Other .416 calibers Many American shooters considered the .416 caliber had become, regrettably, obsolete—despite the fact that ammunition was still loaded for .416 Rigby, and Rigby in London were making the rifles for it. American interest was awakened in 1988 when the .416 Remington Magnum cartridge was produced. It had a belted rimless case that was simply 8mm

Rem Mag necked up to hold a 400 grain (25.9 g) bullet, which it powered to 2,400 fps (732 mps) for an energy of 5,115 ft lb (6,931 joules); little more than that of the Rigby cartridge.

The following year, Weatherby announced its own .416 Weatherby cartridge, which also had a belted rimless case similar to that of Remington's. The .416 Weatherby also used a 400 grain bullet but gave a higher velocity of 2,700 fps (823 mps) and an energy of 6,476 ft lb (8,755 joules) that considerably improved penetration of angled shots on thick-skinned game.

.500 Rimless Jeffrey For many years the .500 Rimless Jeffrey was the most powerful cartridge available for bolt action magazine rifles. Like .425 Westley Richards it actually had a rebated rim of smaller diameter than the case to fit the bolt face in a Mauser action. The cartridge is, in fact, identical to the German 12.7 x 70 (500) Schuler, both having the same bullet weight: 535 grains (34.7 g), and the same ballistics: a muzzle velocity of 2,400 fps (732 mps) and an energy of 6,800 ft lb (9,214 joules). The cartridge has been used extensively in Africa in both guises. Jeffrey designed a .400 bore cartridge, known as .404 Rimless Nitro Express for his magazine rifles. The .404 Jeffrey has been used by RCCM in Canada as the base case for their Imperial Magnum cartridges.

.505 Gibbs Rimless Magnum Ballistically slightly inferior to the .500 Jeffrey, .505 Gibbs

was introduced just before World War I, and established the unfounded reputation of being a bone breaker when fired.

European cartridges There have been a large number of high powered "European" (as opposed to British and American cartridges) produced for Mauser action rifles. Some, like 12.7 x 70 Schuler and 7mm Mauser, were interchangeable with Imperial calibers. For example, 7mm Mauser is the same as .275 Rigby. Others are unique: Wilhelm Brenneke designed many cartridges for his own Mauser action rifles in Germany before World War I; between the wars E. A. Van Hofe did the same. The most powerful of the Brenneke cartridges is 9.3 x 64, which was available in a number of loadings. The most potent of these has a 293 grain (19.0 g) bullet traveling at 2,660 fps (811 mps) which translates as an energy of 4,640 ft lb (6,287 joules).

Norma in Sweden introduced its own belted magnum cartridge in 1960 that had slightly better performance than the .300 H&H Magnum. The caliber, .308 Norma Magnum uses an Imperial designation in the same way that Lapua does with its sniping/high performance cartridge .338 Lapua Magnum, although the Lapua cartridge does have an additional standard Metric listing, 8.6 x 71mm .308 Norma Magnum has slightly less power than .300 Weatherby Magnum; the conventional rimmed .338 Lapua Magnum is comparable to .340 Weatherby.

MAGNUM FORCES

IN THE 1930s there was a move to increase the powder charge to give the bullet more speed and power, and the so-called Magnum cartridge was introduced. Since the diameter of the bullets is about the same, the Magnum cases are made slightly longer than the normal cartridge so that they cannot be loaded into weapons that are not designed to take Magnum loads. There have been attempts to introduce what might be called nonstandard calibers such as .41in, and several persuasive arguments have been put forward to suggest that it would certainly be a useful round for police forces which could utilize its strong stopping power.

CUSTOMIZED BULLETS

THE .700 is not the only double rifle made by Holland & Holland; it will build a rifle to order in virtually any standard caliber specified by the customer. Each rifle is hand-made and produced to an exact specification, the size of the action and overall weight being matched to the caliber. The method of construction is similar to that of a double-barreled side-by-side shotgun, but the action strength is improved to cope with the rifle's higher pressures. The double bite in the receiver, which holds the action closed during firing, is supplemented by an additional "hidden" bite between the ejectors which engages in the breech-face. A rounded thickening of the action known as the bolster (just below the chambers) adds rigidity, and the hammer springs are reversed in the back-action, sidelock trigger group to eliminate the need to remove metal in highly stressed areas.

LEFT
The original cartridges fired a 1,000 grain bullet with a muzzle energy of 9,050 ft lbs (12,263 joules).

BELOW
Each .700 is handmade to an exact specification, the size of the action and overall weight being matched to the caliber.

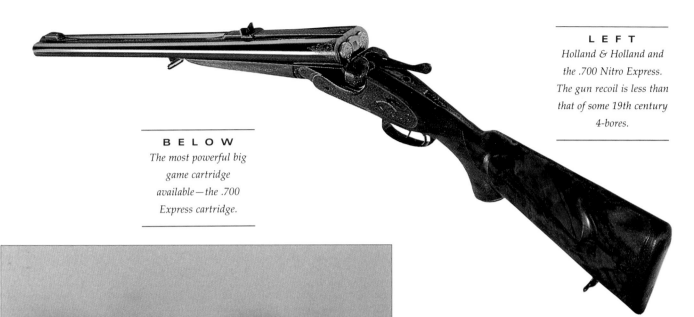

B E L O W
*The most powerful big
game cartridge
available—the .700
Express cartridge.*

remove metal in highly stressed areas.

The new .700 Express cartridge is designed for a new double rifle produced by Holland & Holland and is now the most powerful big game cartridge available. The story behind the .700 Express began in 1974 when Holland & Holland ended production of .60 Nitro Express double rifles. They believed that the demand for such large calibres was at an end, and with great fanfare announced the sale of the "The Last H&H .600 Express". During the 1980s Holland & Holland were asked to build another .600 Express by Mr William Feldstein of Beverly Hills, California. They refused, because they had made a commitment to the purchaser of the previous .600 rifle that his would be their last, and unless he sold it back to them they would not make any more. Feldstein then discussed the problem with Jim Bell of Bell Basic Brass, a speciality cartridge case manufacturer. They came up with the idea of an even bigger cartridge than .600, and Holland & Holland agreed to build rifles in .700 Nitro Express. The first rifle was completed in 1989 and weighted 19 lb (8.5 kg). The original cartridges fired a 1000 grain bullet propelled by 215 grains (13.9 g) of IMR 4831 powder to a velocity of 202 fps (616 mps) and a muzzle energy of 9050 ft lb (12,263 joules). The gun is heavy but the well-balanced weight ensures that the recoil is not excessive – just over 136 ft lb (184 joules) – less than that of some 19th-century 4-bores.

SMOKELESS POWDER AND CASELESS CARTRIDGES

THE FINAL leap in ammunition technology came with the production of high-pressure "smokeless" powders made from nitrated wood, cotton or glycerine. With little or no fouling from powder residue, smokeless powders made self-loading firearms possible. Nitro-cellulos, guncotton, and nitroglycerine-based propellants also pushed bullet velocities to a different level. Without using big heavy bullets, it was difficult to reach speeds of much more than 450 mps (1,500 fps) using black powder in short handgun and rifle barrels. However, with smokeless powders, velocities of 1,200 mps (4,000 fps) could be attained using small caliber bullets which gave the advantage of lighter weight, lower cost, and a flatter trajectory.

A CARTRIDGE WITHOUT A CASE

However, the greatest change was to appear in Germany. When the Federal German Army was formed in the 1950s, it adopted a Heckler & Koch 7.672mm rifle, which, though it employed a delayed blowback system, was very different from that used by the contemporary French FA-MASFI. It depended upon two rollers locking the breech block momentarily until forced out of engagement by the breech pressure. Following that, the Germans then sat down to consider what their future rifle might be. Among their demands was the usual "high hit probability," which simply meant a better chance of hitting the target in fleeting snap-shot situations. A three-round burst of fire for one trigger pressure was an obvious solution, but a conventional rifle with this system was a dubious proposition in their eyes; the first of the three rounds goes toward the target, but, immediately, the muzzle of the rifle begins to lift due to the recoil force and the second shot goes high, the third shot going higher still. What was needed was a rate of fire for those three shots which was simply impossible for a conventional weapon.

The solution, devised by Heckler & Koch, was to do away with the conventional brass-cased cartridge and adopt a cartridge without a case—in other words a chunk of propellant with a bullet. On firing, there would be no case to extract and eject from the gun before loading a fresh round, so that reloading could begin immediately and thus the rate of fire would be speeded up. Development of this, the G11 rifle, began in 1969 with the aim of placing it in service in 1990. The rifle is gas-operated, but uses an entirely novel breech system. The chamber is bored into a circular block mounted behind the barrel. The magazine slides into the rifle above the barrel and feeds the cartridge nose-first downward into the chamber; this then turns through 90 degrees to align with the barrel and the round is fired. The chamber block turns back to accept a new round, back to align and so on. However, when the three round burst is selected the action speeds up; the first round is fired and the barrel and breech begin recoiling inside the plastic casing of the rifle. During the recoil movement, the second round is loaded and then the third round. Only after this does the recoil movement come to a stop with the firer feeling the recoil blow against his shoulder; the three shots sound like one, since they are fired at a rate of 2,200 rounds per minute. As a result, the rifle remains aligned with the target for all three rounds and the three bullets close to each other at the target; if the first one misses, the other two will probably hit.

The rifle did go into service, as promised, in 1990, but only for Special Forces. The same year saw German reunification and the government found itself in need of cash to rehabilitate the east German economy. Something had to go, and as part of the "peace dividend" the G11 rifle was a victim; instead of rearming the entire German Army, the program has been shelved for the foreseeable future.

ABOVE
The Heckler & Koch G11 caseless rifle took 21 years to develop.

RIGHT
The caseless cartridges developed for the Heckler & Koch G11

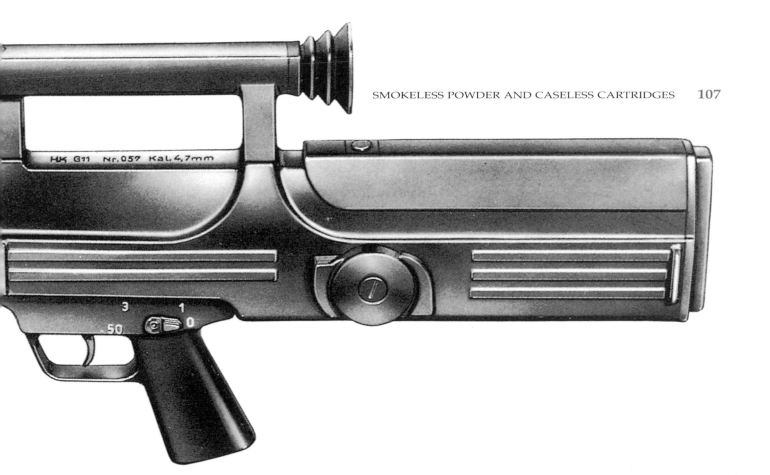

MUZZLE ENERGY AND RELATIVE STOPPING POWER

How do we compare the power of the various types of modern ammunition and the firearms they are to be used in? One of the most popular measurements for comparison is muzzle energy. This is the theoretical energy of the projectile calculated from the square of its velocity, multiplied by the bullet weight, and divided by twice the acceleration of gravity. Muzzle energy is measured in foot-pounds or joules. (One joule being equal to .738 ft lb.) By using the conversion factor 450240, which incorporates the acceleration due to gravity and the conversion of a bullet weight in grains to weight in pounds, the following formula gives muzzle energy in ft lb:

$$\text{Muzzle energy} = \frac{\text{Velocity (fps) squared x Bullet weight (grains)}}{450240}$$

Muzzle energy is not the only factory in assessing power of a cartridge. The primary objective of a bullet is to kill or incapacitate its target, and the diameter of a bullet also plays a significant part in this. A big bullet traveling at a moderate speed seems to have better "stopping power" than a small bullet traveling at high speed—even with the same notional muzzle energy. A classic example of this is the comparison between the 9mm Luger and .45 ACP pistol cartridges. The 9mm Luger ammunition fires a .353in (9mm) diameter, 115 grain (7.45 g) jacketed bullet at approximately 1150 fps (350 mps) giving a muzzle energy of 338 ft lb (458 joules). Some .45 ACP service ammunition (hardball) fires a .451in (11.5mm) diameter, 230 grain (14.9 g) bullet of 800 fps (243 mps) for 327 ft lb (443 joules). On the basis of muzzle energy it is claimed that 9mm Luger is more powerful, yet in accurately documented fire fights, the .45

ABOVE

Hollowpoint bullets and ammunition are available in most handgun calibers from .22 to .45 for sport or survival. In theory the hollow nose mushrooms on impact, imparting most of the energy into the target. In practice, high velocities are needed for significant and effective expansion.

BELOW

By modifying the bullet design, performance can be improved in the 9mm/.357 calibers, as shown by Lapua's Controlled Expansion Police Projectile (CEPP).

ACP hardball has proved time and time again to be far more effective at killing or incapacitating opponents with much fewer shots. One commentator noted that this was because "big holes let in a lot of air and let out a lot of blood."

Observations on relative stopping power have led some gunwriters to propose other scales to compare the power of ammunition. One is based on a "relative stopping power index" and is actually calculated for specific bullet designs. Hollowpoint bullets, for example, expand as they hit flesh, increasing the cross-sectional area of impact. The amount of expansion is affected by velocity, however, and the faster the bullet, the greater the expansion. Hollowpoints work well at rifle velocities of 2,000 fps (609 mps) or more, but their performance is variable at handgun velocities of 1,000 fps (305 mps) often with incomplete expansion or plugging of the hollow nose as it passes through clothing.

Big game hunters in Africa use the Taylor Knock Out table in calculating the potential effectiveness of a cartridge against dangerous game. The TKO table simply multiplies bullet weight by velocity and bore diameter and divides the result by 7,000 to give a manageable figure. (7,000 being the number of grains there are in a 1 lb weight). Applying the TKO table to the 9mm/.45 comparison, rates 9mm Luger at 6.7 units and the .45 ACP at 11.85, making the ACP nearly 80 percent more effective.

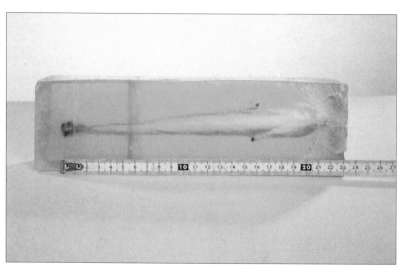

PUTTING POWER TO USE

ANY DISCUSSION on the most powerful fire-arms in the world must take into account the type of weapon used, and the design and use of the firearm. There are also physical limits to the pressure some breech designs can obtain. Of course the ammunition itself is the key to power.

Consider, for example, the .308 Winchester rifle cartridge (also known as 7.62mm NATO). Until recently this was the standard issue service rifle cartridge for NATO armies. It is also a very effective hunting round, typically firing a 150 grain (9.7 g) bullet at 2,860 fps (872 mps) giving an energy of 2,725 ft lb (3,690 joules) and a TKO index of 18.9. In normal service or hunting rifles, the cartridge has moderate recoil and adequate but not excessive energy. Although "powerful" it cannot compare with the .460 Weatherby Magnum dangerous game cartridge, which generates over 8,000 ft lb (10,840 joules)

with a .458in (11.6mm) diameter 500 grain (32.4 gram) bullet travelling at 2,700 fps (822 mps) with a TKO index of 89.

A handgun made for .308 Winchester with a shorter barrel would lose approximately 500 fps (152 mps) off the velocity. Despite this the muzzle energy would still be around 1,850 ft lb (2,507 joules), 150 ft lb (203 joules) more than the .454 Casull—which is the world's most powerful production revolver cartridge today.

The perceived power is also relevant to both the shooter and the target. For example, if a .44 Special revolver cartridge is fired in a 20oz (567 gram) revolver there is heavy recoil and the handgun torques violently in the hand. Put the same ammunition in an 80 oz (2268 gram) rifle chambered for .44 and the recoil would be slight.

Handguns can be viewed as powerful when they reach muzzle energies of more than 350 ft

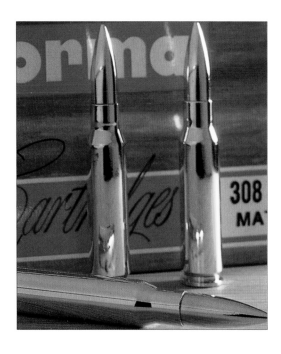

LEFT
.308 Winchester is exactly the same caliber as 7.62mm NATO, until recently the issue ammunition for NATO forces. It is being replaced by .223 Remington (5.56mm NATO) for general use but retained for sniping.

BELOW
The .454 Casull fires the most powerful revolver cartridges made today.

lb (406 joules), ideally coupled with a barrel bore of .40in (10mm) and above. Rifles cannot be regarded as powerful unless they have muzzle energies of more than 2,000 ft lb (2,710 joules) and a barrel bore diameter of .243in (6mm).

DIVERSITY

The improvements in ammunition in the 19th century coupled with better grade steels for gun parts spawned a number of smallarms designs. In the 20th century these have been consolidated into three groups of rifles and three groups of handguns. Each type has enough distinctive qualities to merit a chapter in itself; however, it is worth while to compare the designs briefly at this stage to see where most power can be obtained.

Revolvers The age of powerful revolvers began when Colt made the 1847 Walker. One of the most famous revolvers is another Colt product, the 1873 Single Action Army, known as the Peacemaker. The Peacemaker was produced in a range of cartridge calibers, but the most popular was the .45 Colt, which used a black powder charge. A formidable cartridge that is still with us today as a smokeless round, the .45 Colt was the model for the current most powerful production revolver round, the .454 Casull.

Self-loading pistols Self-loading pistols became feasible with the introduction of smokeless propellants just before the turn of the century. With heavy reciprocating parts they soon became unpleasant to fire as ammunition power increased. The physical size of ammunition was limited by the size of the grip; the most compact designs used a clip magazine to hold ammunition, which was slipped into the butt of the pistol. Western military powers soon settled on the 9mm Luger and .45 ACP calibers as satisfactory for defensive use in self-loading handguns. They also used them for offensive purposes in machine pistols and submachine-guns during World War II. Civilians designed more powerful calibers for sporting use in the second half of the 20th century. The most powerful of these is almost certainly the recently launched .50 AE round for use in the Israeli Desert Eagle pistol, which is sold commercially in the West. This firearm will generate approximately 1,790 ft lb (2,425 joules) of energy with a 300 grain (19.4 g) bullet.

Single-shot handguns In the world of single-shot and bolt-action handguns virtually anything can be produced in terms of power and ballistic performance. Many single-shot pistols are simply shortened rifles with a pistol stock. They are popular for handgun hunting and long-range steel plate target shooting. They are also ideal for "wildcatting," the practice of making new calibers up from existing cartridge cases by increasing or decreasing the bullet diameter, enlarging the case to increase propellant capacity, or shortening the case to give better ballistics from a short barrel (see pages 151–153).

Single-barreled sporting rifles Powerful sporting rifles with a single barrel use a range of different breech types to secure the cartridge during firing. Many of them are repeating arms using a magazine to feed another round into the chamber as the action is cycled. The most popular guns of this type are bolt action, which derive from the German Mauser actions designed in 1898. The earliest high-powered sporting rifles were the Henry/Winchester lever actions, single-shot Martinis, and various falling block actions. Moderately powered sporting rifles are now made with pump- and gas-operated self-

RIGHT
The three handgun cartridges illustrated span the range of pistol power. On the left is 2.7mm Kolibri Auto, a tiny obsolete center-fire pistol round which has less energy than an air pistol (3ft lb). In the center, the .22 LR rimfire cartridge is among the lowest powered of any pistol or rifle ammunition currently made. On the right .454 Casull, derived from .45 Colt, has 30 times the energy of .22 LR and 500 times the energy of 2.7mm Kolibri.

BELOW
Century Arms revolvers are more powerful still, firing big bore vintage and modern rifle cartridges.

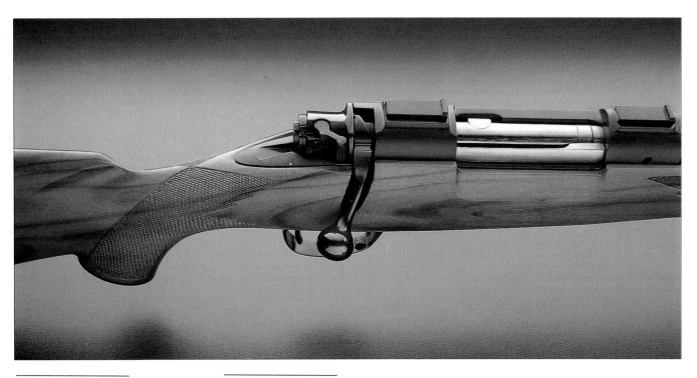

A B O V E

*Kimber rifles feature fine
workmanship and classic
Mauser-type bolt actions.*

B E L O W

*The single-shot
Thompson Center
Contender has
interchangeable barrels*

*which are chambered for a
wide range of handgun
and rifle calibers.*

loading actions but the most powerful use bolt actions which, with .460 Weatherby ammunition, are able to reach 8,000 ft lb (10,840 joules).

Double-barreled sporting rifles Almost entirely British in origin, the double-barreled sporting rifle of today has changed little in appearance from those made at the end of the 19th century. Designed for dangerous game shooting in India and Africa, double-barreled rifles were well-balanced, easy to swing—and utterly reliable. They contained only two cartridges but in the last century the muzzle energy they generated per round with .577 Nitro Express ammunition reached 7,000 ft lb (9,485 joules). Double-barreled rifles are manufactured in even larger calibers today, and their muzzle energies are over 9,000 ft lb (12,200 joules).

High-powered military rifles Military rifles have two applications; for use against enemy personnel, and enemy equipment. Military conflicts at the turn of the century proved that the most effective rifles against personnel had a caliber of around .30in (7.62mm) and a muzzle energy of 2,500 to 3,000 ft lb (3,390–4,065 joules). In this energy range a soldier could penetrate

buildings and unprotected vehicles with high velocity ammunity, shooting accurately at ranges of up to 600 yd (500 m). For volley fire against an advancing horde, ranges of up to 2,000 yd (1,830 m) were used in early conflicts, but bullet-striking energy at that range is minimal

Two of the most famous and effective rounds of both world wars were Great Britain's .303 British, and the US .30-06 Springfield cartridges; both were used in bolt action rifles and automatic machine guns. The .30-60 cartridge was also used in the Garand gas-operated rifle, in 1936—the first self-loading rifle adopted by any army in the world. The advent of light and medium armor on early tanks used in World War I put new demands on the penetrating power required of smallarms and their ammunition. At first, steel-cored bullets were used in conventional rifles to improve penetration, but by the beginning of World War II armor had

been improved and extremely powerful anti-tank rifles with calibers up to .508in (20mm) were developed. The best of these could puncture 1.2in (30mm) of armor with a perpendicular bullet strike. The British .55 Boys round developed in the 1930s had a muzzle energy of 13,722 ft lb (18,593 joules). The 20mm Lahti was even more potent with 37,400 ft lb (50,677 joules) of energy and is still ranked as one of the most powerful weapons that can be fired by one person without beiing mounted on a vehicle.

By the end of the war, tank armor had advanced to the stage where only artillery fire or explosive rockets could cause damage to it, and the half-inch military calibers faded from favor. In recent times, there has been a resurgence of interest in .50 Browning for use as a military sniping round—doubtless because of its high energy and very flat bullet trajectory.

A B O V E
Modern .308 caliber sniping rifles are accurate at ranges of up to 600 yards, and the ammunition can penetrate buildings.

MEASURING MAGNUMS & "SUPERMAGS"

THE SMOKELESS propellants of the turn of the century gave ammunition manufacturers the opportunity to develop high velocity ammunition. This was particularly suited to pistols, where the closed breech prevented the gas loss experienced in revolvers. The Mauser 1896 pistol used a high-powered version of Borchardt's 7.65mm cartridge known as 7.63mm Mauser to propel a light 86 grain bullet to 1,410 ft per second (fps), the fastest commercial handgun round available until the .357 Magnum was introduced for revolvers. In Great Britain in the early 1900s, Hugh Gabbet-Fairfax designed the ill-fated Mars pistol, which fired a 9mm 156 grain bullet at 1,650 fps, developing nearly three times the energy of 9mm Luger or 7.63mm Mauser. The Mars was never adopted for service due to its complexity, size, and recoil, but it demonstrated the power that could now be generated by handgun ammunition using smokeless propellants. High velocities were confined to fairly small bores and light bullets, since pressure drops off very rapidly in large calibers due to the large barrel volume left by the departing bullet. In order to keep up the pressure and attain high velocities, a lot of slow burning propellant is required, which in turn needs a large cartridge case. Too large for butt magazine pistols, which had become the best balanced self-loading pistol layout, it was left to revolver cartridges to make the next advances in velocity and muzzle energy.

MAGNUM REVOLVER CARTRIDGES

.357 Magnum The first modern magnum cartridge, .357 Magnum, was developed in 1935 by Smith & Wesson and Winchester for S&W's heavy frame revolvers. Basically a .38 S&W Special case lengthened by .135in to prevent it being chambered in .38 revolvers, the .357 Magnum cartridge produced three times the muzzle energy of the .38 Special and is now the most popular high velocity revolver round in the world. Originally loaded to push a 158 grain bullet out of an 8¾in revolver barrel at over 1,500 fps, the .357 Magnum has now been backed off in pressure and today factory loadings give 1,200–1,300 fps with a 158 grain bullet, and 1450 fps with a lighter 125 grain bullet.

ABOVE
The .38 S&W revolver cartridge (left) originated around 1877. The improved .38 S&W Special (2nd left) with smokeless powder was introduced in 1902. This itself was stretched in 1935 to give the .357 S&W Magnum (second right), one of the most popular revolver cartridges in use today. A further lengthening of the case in 1983 gave the .357 Maximum (right), which can generate over 1,100ft lb of muzzle energy.

.44 Remington Magnum Twenty years later, Smith & Wesson and Remington produced the .44 Magnum, egged on by Elmer Keith, a bullet designer, hunter, and pistol shooter who had developed a number of high velocity loadings for .44 Special and .45 Colt. Until recently, this was the most powerful handgun cartridge in the world and owes a lot of its notoriety to Clint Eastwood, who in several films of the 1970s and 80s portrayed a fictional San Francisco detective (Harry Callahan) who preferred dealing with low life with the phenomenal stopping power of the .44 Magnum over his issue .357 Magnum. Like the .357 Magnum before it, the .44 Magnum was based on an existing case, the .44 Special; like the .38 Special, the .44 Special was lengthened so that the high pressure round could not be inadvertently used in revolvers made for the low pressure cartridge. The .44 Special itself had grown out of the .44 Russian, when bulky, smokeless powders were first used.

.41 Remington Magnum The recoil and blast of the .44 Magnum was difficult for inexperienced shooters to control, and in 1967 Smith & Wesson introduced a totally new cartridge designed to fill the gap between the .357 and .44 Magnums. The .41 Magnum was conceived as the ultimate law enforcement caliber, but it was not widely adopted; it could only be fired in a heavy, large frame revolver, and the factory ammunition loadings still had considerable recoil, more than many policemen and policewomen would tolerate. The impressive ballistics and accuracy of the round caught the attention of a few American shooters, who successfully used it for handgun hunting. Today Smith & Wesson and Ruger still produces double-action revolvers chambered for .41 Magnum, but their sales are not for law enforcement but to sportsmen.

.32 H&R Magnum Since the Magnum tag seemed to enhance sales of guns and ammunition, in 1984 the Federal Cartridge Company

LEFT
The .41 Magnum was an attempt to produce the "ideal" police revolver cartridge in 1964. The recoil was still too powerful for some officers, but .41 Magnum has been eagerly accepted by handgun hunters as a good hunting round without the blast of .44 Magnum.

introduced the .32 Harrington & Richardson Magnum for the now defunct New England gunmakers Harrington & Richardson. Like the .357 and .44 Magnums, the .32 H&R Magnum was based on the existing .32 Smith & Wesson Long case, lengthened by .155in. Unlike the other Magnums, however, the .32 was loaded to fairly low pressures, comparable with those of the old .38 Special.

.357 Remington Maximum In the search for a super Magnum revolver cartridge, the .357 Magnum was stretched by .3in, and the .357 Remington Maximum was introduced in 1983. Ruger and Dan Wesson produced revolvers chambered for the new caliber, but problems of gas-cutting of the frame in front of the cylinder, and of rapid barrel wear have caused many people to feel that at 1,825 fps with a 158 grain bullet, the safe pressure and velocity limit for a repeating handgun was being exceeded by the .357 Maximum. The round has been eagerly adopted by single shot pistol manufacturers, however, who have no such gas-cutting problems.

.454 Casull The title of "the most powerful production revolver cartridge in the world" now belongs to the .454 Casull. This was developed from the .45 Colt cartridge which had been introduced in the 1873 Peacemaker, and, like the .32, .357, and .44 Magnums, uses a longer and far stronger case than its parent. The .454 Casull was originally named the .454 Magnum Revolver by Dick Casull and Jack Fullmer, its inventors in 1957. However, the Magnum designation seems to gain popularity for the wrong reasons these days, and now that five-shot .454 Casull single action revolvers are being made for the cartridge by Freedom Arms Inc., the production cartridge carries the designer's name instead. Factory ammunition pushes a 260 grain bullet to 1,720 feet per second giving 1,700 ft lb of muzzle energy, nearly twice that of a factory loaded .44 Magnum, and 40 times that of the first rimfire .22s.

.45–70 Government Big bore single action revolvers are now being chambered for .45–70 government, an old parallel-sided black

The most powerful production revolver cartridge now made is the .454 Casull which can develop twice the energy of .44 Magnum when fired from the Freedom Arms Casull.

L E F T

The vintage black powder rifle cartridge, the .45–70 Gov't (center) is now being chambered in big bore single action revolvers. Either side stand the .357 Magnum and .44 Magnum.

powder rifle cartridge used by the US military from 1873 to 1892. While the case is even larger than that of the Casull, it was originally designed for black powder propellant and is not strong enough for Magnum pressures approaching those of the Casull. The .45–70 is not officially classed as a handgun cartridge.

.22 Remington Jet and .256 Winchester Magnum With an aim to developing better Magnum revolver cartridges, both Remington and Winchester played with bottle-necked rounds in 1960–1961 based on the .357 Magnum case. Remington necked down the case to produce the .22 Remington Jet, firing a .223in 50 grain bullet to 2,460 fps from an 8½in Smith & Wesson barrel. Winchester made the .256 Winchester Magnum handgun cartridge, which fired a 60 grain bullet at 2,200 fps that could penetrate a ¼in (6mm) steel plate, but no handgun manufacturer produced a revolver chambered for it. While the fast, light bullet gave high energies with minimal recoil, the tapered, bottle-necked case tended to back out of the cylinder on firing,

locking up the whole gun. Both cartridges are still occasionally chambered in single shot pistols, but no longer in revolvers.

.357 Magnum The high energies recently achieved by the custom-made revolvers and handmade ammunition tend to overshadow the advances made in high pressure revolver ammunition between the two World Wars. It was shortly after World War I that American law enforcement agencies began dealing with the increasing rise of organized crime. They requested handguns with greater penetration than their standard issue revolvers and .38 Special ammunition, Smith & Wesson responded by manufacturing a revolver in 1930 based on their heavy N frame used for .44 and .45 revolvers and chambered for .38 Special. Ammunition companies made special high velocity .38 ammunition for use in the tough frames and called it .38–44 S & W Special. The noted writer and ammunition experimenter Philip B. Sharpe started developing high velocity loadings for the .38–44 and before long Smith & Wesson became interested in his results. Along with Winchester they produced a new caliber in 1934, .357 Magnum, which in time has become

one of the most popular law enforcement and personal defense rounds in existence. The cartridge was ⅛in longer than .38 Special but shared the size same case diameter and rim so that a revolver chambered for .357 Magnum could also chamber and fire lower powered .38 Special ammunition. The first Smith & Wesson .357 Magnum revolver was completed in April 1935 and was presented to J. Edgar Hoover, then director of the FBI. The N frame S&W .357 Magnum revolver was later given the model

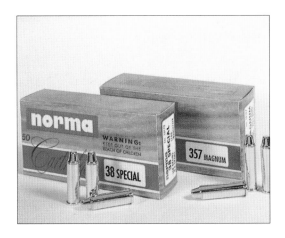

number 27, and is still in production today.

With improvements in the quality of steel it had been possible to produce medium-frame revolvers that can safely fire .357 Magnum ammunition. The original Winchester loads claimed a velocity from 8¾in (222mm) barrel of 1,515 fps (472 mps) with a 158 grain (10.2 g) bullet, that gave a muzzle energy of 805 ft lb (109 joules), compared with 255 ft lb (345 joules) for standard 158 grain .38 Special cartridges. Since the introduction of .357 Magnum the pressures and velocities have been reduced in the United States and the best energy Winchester now

A B O V E
.357 Magnum revolvers   *world for target shooting,*
are the most popular high   *defence, and hunting*
powered handguns in the   *small game.*

available is 583 ft lb (790 joules) with a 125 grain (8.1 g) bullet traveling at 1,450 fps (422 joules). In Europe RWS and Norma still load up to the old standard, with Norma claiming 1,490 fps (454 mps) with a 158 grain bullet.

Virtually every center-fire revolver manufacturer in the world produces a handgun chambered for .357 Magnum. In the United States, Smith & Wesson lists seven double-action model types in stainless and blued steel, with a total of 20 model/barrel length options. Sturm Turger lists 14 versions of its double-action Model GP100 and six versions of its single-action Blackhawk. Colt sells blue and stainless steel versions of its double-action King Cobra and Python Models. Double-action .357 revolvers are made by a variety of firms around the world: in Germany by Weirauch and Korth, in Spain by Llama and Astra, in Brazil by Taurus and Rossi, and in France by Manurhin.

.357 Maximum Heavy .357in caliber bullets at high velocity have a very flat trajectory and have become popular for the sport of metallic silhouette shooting, where steel targets in the shape of animals and birds are shot at extended

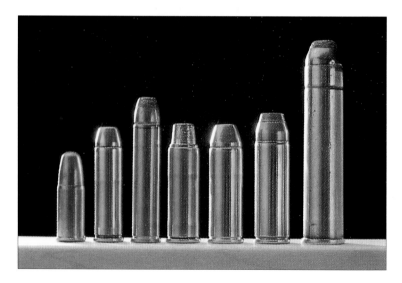

ABOVE

Apart from the .38 Smith & Wesson cartridge on the far left, the rounds illustrated can all be regarded as powerful in revolvers. The complete range (from the left) is: .38 Smith & Wesson .357 Magnum, .357 Maximum, .41 Magnum, .44 Magnum, .454 Casull, and .50–110 Gov't.

ranges out to 250 yards. In order to exploit the superior exterior ballistics of .357 bullets, Sturm Ruger and Remington jointly developed the .357 Maximum, which was essentially an elongated .357 Magnum cartridge that ran velocities in vented test barrels of 1,825 fps (556 mps) with 158 grain bullets. The revolvers made by Ruger in 1983 and Dan Wesson in 1984 chambered for .357 Maximum suffered from excessive gas cutting of the frame and barrel, and the Ruger was eventually discontinued. The performance of the round was also disappointing, falling 200 fps (61 mps) short of the test barrel velocities when fired in production handguns. The potential of the cartridge has been developed in single-shot pistols however, where there are no cylinder-to-chamber gaps, and therefore no loss of pressure or gas cutting.

.41 Magnum Despite the success of the .357 and .44 Magnum cartridges, there was a need for an intermediate revolver cartridge for law enforcement, with more stopping power than the .357,

but without the blast and high recoil of the .44. The result was the .41 S&W Magnum introduced in 1964 along with the Smith & Wesson Model 57 revolver. Nevertheless, the .41 Magnum proved to be too powerful for many police officers. The handgun was on the same large N frame used for the .44 Magnum model 29, and was rather bulky to carry. As a result .41 Magnum was not a commercial success for law enforcement, but it was enthusiastically received by some sportsmen as a handgun hunting cartridge because the lighter bullet gave it better penetration than .44 Magnum with up to 20 per cent less recoil. Muzzle velocity for a 210 grain (13.6 g) bullet in .41 Magnum ranges from 1,300–1,500 fps (396–457 mps), giving muzzle energies from 790 to 1,050 ft lb (1,070–1,423 joules). Smith & Wesson still produces two .41 Magnum revolvers, the original Model 57 in blue steel and the 657 in stainless steel. Ruger chambers its Redhawk and Blackhawk revolvers for .41 Magnum and Dan Wesson has also produced models for the caliber.

WINCHESTER MAGNUMS

CALIBER	BULLET WT		MUZZLE VELOCITY		MUZZLE ENERGY	
	GRAINS	(GRAMS)	FPS	(MPS)	FT LBS	(JOULES)
.264 Win Mag	100	6.5	3700	1128	3040	4119
	140	9.1	3200	975	3180	4309
.300 Win Mag	150	9.7	3400	1036	3865	5237
	180	11.7	3070	936	3740	5068
.338 Win Mag	200	13.0	3000	914	4000	5420
	250	16.2	2700	823	4050	5488
	300	19.4	2450	747	4000	5420
.458 Win Mag	500	32.4	2130	649	5040	6829
	510	33.1	2130	649	5140	6965

Winchester produces a considerable range of belted rimless cartridges with the Magnum tag, which has displaced the old term "Express" for high-velocity and high-powered cartridges. In addition to ammunition, Winchester makes the Model 70 Sporter and Super Express bolt action rifle for its own and other calibers. The performance data on the belted Winchester Magnums is as follows:

The Supermags The sport of shooting long-range metallic targets also created another range of high-powered cartridges and revolvers jointly developed by Elgin Gates of the IHMSA (International Handgun Metallic Silhouette Association) and Dan Wesson Arms. The first was the .357 SuperMag, which used a slightly longer cartridge case than .357 Maximum and shot 180 grain and 200 grain (11.66 & 13 g) bullets at the same speeds as 158 grain bullets out of .357 Magnum. The interchangeable barrels of the Dan Wesson 6-shot revolvers soon had experimenters unscrewing the .357 Super-Mag barrels and replacing them with re-threaded .44 Magnum tubes. The cylinder chambers were bored out to take a long version of .44 Magnum ammunition made from .444 Marlin or .30–40 Krag cases that were lathe-turned at the base and trimmed at the mouth to 1.620in (41mm) in length. This high velocity

Remington Arms Company in Wilmington, Delaware, has a similar range of belted magnum cartridges and chamber its Model 700 rifles for these and other calibers. The Remington Model 700 is used by the US Army as a sniping rifle. The ballistics data of the Remington belted magnums is as follows:

RIGHT
Tikka Model 65 chambered for 7mm Rem Magnum.

REMINGTON MAGNUMS

CALIBER	BULLET WT		MUZZLE VELOCITY		MUZZLE ENERGY	
	GRAINS	(GRAMS)	FPS	(MPS)	FT LBS	(JOULES)
6.5mm Rem Mag	120	7.8	3210	978	2745	3720
7mm Rem Mag	140	9.1	3175	968	3313	4489
	150	9.7	3110	948	3221	4365
	175	11.3	2860	872	3178	4306
8mm Rem Mag	185	12.0	3080	939	3896	5279
	220	14.3	2830	863	3912	5301
.350 Rem Mag	200	13.0	2710	826	3261	4419
.416 Rem Mag	400	26.0	2400	732	5115	6931

wildcat cartridge was dubbed the .44 UltraMag and could reach velocities of almost 1,600 fps (488 mps) with 305 grain (19.8 g) bullets out of a 6in (152mm) barrel and a muzzle energy of 1,734 ft lb (2,350 joules). By 1989 the various types of the .44 UltraMag were legitimized for use by IHMSA competitors in a version known as the .445 SuperMag, which joined the already established .357 SuperMag and .375 SuperMag. The latter was also a new IHMSA caliber made from shortened .375 Winchester cases trimmed to 1.610in (40.9mm) like the rest of Gates's SuperMags. Dan Wesson made 8in and 10in barreled double-action revolvers for the new calibers and the IHMSA produced new cartridge cases that did not require trimming and turning. No factory produces complete ammunition since the competitors in IHMSA "shoots" all hand-load their own rounds, finetuning them for accuracy in their own revolvers.

HIGH-POWERED SPORTING RIFLES

THE WORLD of the double-barreled rifle is a long way removed from that of the sporting bolt action rifle or military smallarm. The power that can be achieved by the double rifle is immense and devastating, and that is why it is used in Africa and India for the pursuit of big game. A standing marksman will attempt to shoot from distances of 100 yards (91 meters) right down to a few paces when hunting such animals as elephants, rhinoceros, lion, and buffalo. The hunter, equipped with a double rifle, has an unrivaled combination of raw energy and insurance in the event of a cartridge misfiring or simply missing a fast-moving target; with a double rifle, a second shot is available immediately with no need to work a bolt.

The origins of the big doubles lie in the fine English sporting shotguns of the 19th century.

In fact, the companies that craft the latter today also manufacture first class double-barreled shotguns.

The demand for double rifles dropped off between the wars as the British Empire was broken up and reduced in size, and the recession of the 1930s reduced disposable incomes. Moreover, big caliber bolt action rifles cost a lot less than double rifles, and provided the shot was placed accurately were just as effective. Telescopic sights became popular for the smaller bore bolt action rifles but they did not catch on with the shooters of double rifles. The telescope added weight and was slow to use, and the change in balance of 'scope-equipped doubles also badly affected their handling. The introduction of the single trigger was also regarded as a backward step by the seasoned hunter who preferred double triggers. Above all else, a

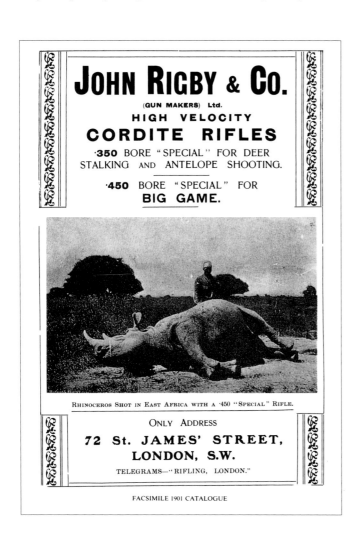

FACSIMILE 1901 CATALOGUE

Combination guns were frowned upon in England, but are popular in continental Europe, especially with "superposed" barrels, one above the other.

dangerous game rifle has to be reliable, and there is nothing more reliable than a double rifle, each barrel having its own independent lockwork and trigger. On many sets of double triggers, the front one is hinged so it will not bruise the trigger finger during recoil when the second barrel is fired.

In many respects the double rifle had reached the peak of its development just prior to World War I. Indeed, the firearms produced today by Holland & Holland, Rigby, and Westley Richards would be instantly recognizable to a hunter setting out for the Cape of Good Hope in 1900. The main change to the big bore game rifle since then is principally cosmetic, with the degree and complexity of the engraving changing as personal tastes have altered. Today a best grade, quality double rifle costs from $40,000 (£25,000) upward and will take up to three years to make. High quality gold inlaid engraving will increase its price, and rifles are now being ordered as works of art rather than tools for killing. One of the world's leading "virtuoso" engravers is Ken

Hunt, who has a three-year waiting list for his work. Some of his creations evoke a bygone age of craftsmanship.

Regulation Much of the cost in the manufacture of a double rifle is incurred in the regulation of the barrels. In order to give both barrels the same point of impact at a given distance, they have to be assembled on the action and stock to be test-fired. A wedge between the barrels at the muzzle is tapped in and adjusted until the fall of shot is the same for each barrel. It can be a long process, sometimes involving separating the barrels and rejoining them if they cannot be brought in line with wedges. The rifle must then be used with ammunition of the same bullet weight and ballistics as that used during regulation.

Paradox barrels In the last century it was not uncommon for dual purpose firearms to be made, which would fire shot or bullet. Some had two sets of barrels, one pair smooth for shot, the other rifled for the solid projectile. Dual-purpose Paradox barrels made under Fosbery's patent could fire both, since they were smooth for most of their length with a rifled choke for the last few inches of barrel. Of the Paradox, W. W. Greener wrote: "They have the accuracy and force of the heavy rifle combined with the lightness and handiness of a shotgun. Firing black powder and a conical bullet at 100 yards, diagrams measuring about 4in by 3in can be obtained. Muzzle velocity of the 12-bore varies from 1,050 to 1,200 feet per second, with a striking energy at 100 yards of 1722 to 1822 ft lb according to load and bullet used."

Combination guns Combination guns were made by English gunmakers in the last century. They consisted of an action with one rifle barrel and one shotgun barrel fitted alongside each other. They gave a hunter the option of a rifle's single-shot power and accuracy for boar or deer, or the shotgun's pellet pattern for wing shooting. Despite these benefits the combination gun was frowned upon in England since it suggested that the owner could not afford both a rifle and a shotgun! In any event the combination did not perform as well as the dedicated firearms, having a worse balance than a shotgun, but more recoil than a rifle. In continental Europe, where there is very restricted ownership of firearms, combination guns which have a rifle barrel under a shotgun tube are still very much in demand. Spanish, German, and Italian gunmakers continue to produce combination pieces with a rifle bore of up to 9.3mm.

Immense 4-bores The first double-barreled big game guns were smooth-bored percussion pieces of immense size, with barrel diameters of 1.052in (26.7mm) for 4-bores, .835in (21.2mm) for 8-bores, and .775in (19.7mm) for 10-bores. The bore scale was derived from the number of round lead balls of the bore diameter that would weight 1 lb. A 4-bore ball would therefore weigh ¼lb (113.4 g); an 8-bore ⅛ lb (56.7 g); and a 10-bore ¹⁄₁₀ lb (43.7 g). Even after the invention of the metallic breech-loading cartridge the big bore rifles were still popular because of their increased potency. Bullet weights were as heavy as 1,882 grains (122 g) in 4-bores, leaving

A B O V E
The two leading British manufacturers of sidelock double rifles, Holland & Holland and Rigby, both

have distinctive appearances to their actions.

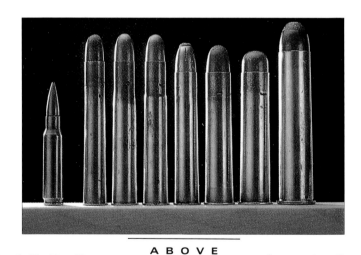

A B O V E
Most double rifle calibers existed before World War I, with the exception of Holland & Holland's 700 NE which was made in

1989. Just a few double rifle Nitro Express cartridges are shown, with a .308 Winchester bolt action rifle cartridge

for comparison. From the left: 308 Win, 450 NE, 500–465 NE, 470 NE, 500 NE, 577 NE, 600 NE, 700 NE.

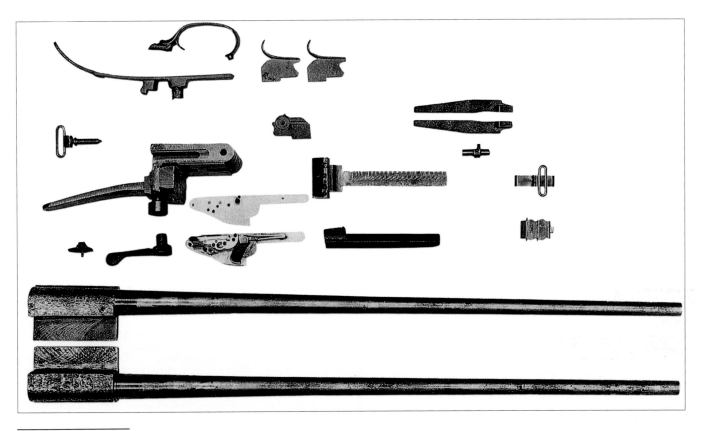

the muzzle at 1,450 fps (442 mps) with an energy of 8,832 ft lb (11,968 joules). The 8-bore proved to be a favorite cartridge for thick-skinned game because it had better penetration than the 4-bore, more muzzle energy than the 10-bore, and a flatter trajectory than both.

Express rifles As the quality of black powder propellant improved toward the middle of the 19th century, so the calibers of hunting rifles were reduced and the velocity of the bullet increased, creating the description "Express." The name was a shortening of "Express Train," a marketing tag used in 1856 by Purdey for his percussion rifles made for South Africa. These were renowned for their long "point blank" range, or flat trajectory, in that virtually the same aim could be taken at 100 yd (91 m) and at 25 yd (23 m) with minimal difference in the point of impact. Compared to the modern high velocity small caliber rifle the trajectory of the Express had a curvature like a rainbow, but was considered a substantial improvement for the open African lains. The term "Express" was retained for high velocity, breech-loading,

cartridge firing rifles. For some years the .577 Express 2¾in cartridge loaded with black powder was regarded as a fine caliber for big game hunting. The bullet weight of between 500 and 700 grains (32.4 and 45.4 g) delivered up to 4,700 ft lb (6,369 joules) of energy at the muzzle, and a striking energy of approximately 3,500 ft lb (4743 joules) at 100 yards. When smokeless propellants became commonplace in the 1890s the .577 case was lengthened to 3in (76.2mm)) and loaded with 100 grains (6.5 g) of cordite behind a 750 grain (48.6 g) bullet. The performance of the new .577 Nitro Express cartridge was much improved with a muzzle velocity up to 2,050 fps (625 mps) giving a muzzle energy of 7,000 ft lb (9,485 joules) and a striking energy at 100 yards of 5,680 ft lb (7,697 joules). While this would flatten an elephant, it was regarded as overkill for other quarry and a range of other calibers was devised. It was common for hunters to have a selection of bore rifles at their disposal. From 1880 to 1910 the range of big bore cartridges for double rifles mushroomed and they were available in a variety of high performance calibers.

HOOKED ON HANDGUNS AND RIFLES

Acalifornian examines his new purchases, a pair of 18th-century flintlock dueling pistols in their hand-made case. Outside are the familiar trappings of the modern age—jumbo jets, fast food, and traffic reports—but for a few moments the collector is a distant world of powdered wigs, intrigue, and wounded honor. A similar feeling transports a German—new owner of an original Winchester 73—to the frontier justice of the American West.

Romance is not the only reason to collect rifles and handguns, but few would deny their associations with memorable historical eras. Rarity and high quality workmanship make them as collectable as any other antiques. Prices have already soared for many pieces, but the knowledgeable can still afford to build collections.

Replicas are also popular, allowing enthusiasts the chance to try target shooting with period weapons. Other marksmen prefer the latest in single-shot handguns, "wildcat" ammunition and rifles, and other innovations in the continuing quest for accuracy and precision. Collectors, target shooters, or simple enthusiasts have helped keep alive a passion that was born more than six centuries ago.

BUILDING A COLLECTION

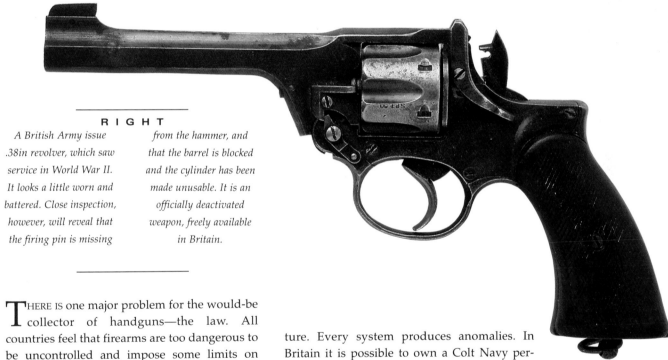

RIGHT

A British Army issue .38in revolver, which saw service in World War II. It looks a little worn and battered. Close inspection, however, will reveal that the firing pin is missing from the hammer, and that the barrel is blocked and the cylinder has been made unusable. It is an officially deactivated weapon, freely available in Britain.

There is one major problem for the would-be collector of handguns—the law. All countries feel that firearms are too dangerous to be uncontrolled and impose some limits on ownership. The one general exception made is in the matter of antiques, for lawmakers feel that the antique weapon does not pose a threat. Most countries allow a collector to keep as many antique firearms as desired, although a few insist that they be registered. The difficulty lies in defining the word antique—and for every definition, it is possible to find exceptions!

Attempts have been made to define antique firearms by the type of action, by the type of ammunition used, and by the date of manufac-ture. Every system produces anomalies. In Britain it is possible to own a Colt Navy percussion revolver made in 1852 but not a copy made in Italy in 1982, but apart from the materials and some modifications for the purpose of manufacture, they are identical. It is assumed by the lawmakers that if somebody purchases a modern copy it is because they plan to fire it. In some countries of Europe the Snider rifle is regarded as an antique, but in others it is not. Some countries do not allow private individuals to own handguns that use military caliber ammunition, so that in some countries one may not

R I G H T
These may look like a Luger 08 pistol and a P38, but they are, in fact, totally harmless copies. A large range of such "models" is available, many of which are made to fire blanks, and most are so realistic that they can be identified as replicas only when they are handled. Some are "soft air" weapons, which fire a harmless plastic pellet.

own a pistol that fires 9mm Parabellum ammunition. However, if the cartridge case and breech are slightly modified the ammunition is no longer the same as the military cartridge and it is legal to own the gun. A British citizen may buy certain firearms abroad but may not take them home unless a special permit is obtained. The latest method being introduced in Britain is to declare that if a particular kind of ammunition is no longer available, the weapon with which it was used may be considered an antique. While any relaxation in the law restricting ownership is welcome, the use of ammunition types as a guideline is going to make life very confusing and difficult for those who have to enforce the regulations.

There is one way of acquiring handguns that requires no license, certificate, or other legal requirement and that is to collect deactivated guns. In order to comply with the law, in Britain and some other countries, firearms can be rendered safe and incapable of firing. Externally they appear unchanged, but firing pins are removed, barrels blocked and sundry other

changes made so they cannot, at least in theory, be reconverted. These deactivated weapons are not cheap, and most shooters and collectors do not approve of the changes made since the gun is ruined. However, there are those who argue that the process gives the enthusiast a chance to acquire items such as machine guns that would otherwise be totally unobtainable. In some countries the deactivation is much more fundamental and obvious. There is no doubt that there is a demand for such items, certainly in Britain, for the number of deactivated weapons that has been sold is very high indeed.

In the United States, laws vary from state to

**O P P O S I T E ,
T O P**
These small vest pocket double barreled-pistols are usually referred to as Derringers and were produced by many of the big manufacturers. they were available in single and double barrel versions and the usual caliber was .41in but other calibers were produced. These are from one of the smaller firearm manufacturers.

R I G H T
An engraving from the British publication The Graphic, *dating from 1881. It is interesting to see the traditional shooting position of the period. The bent arm was adequate for revolvers but not forself-loading pistols.*

state, although there are some federal laws that apply to all the states.

With so many possible legal combinations and opinions the best advice to be given must be make sure that you inform yourself of the law for your area, state or country before even attempting to acquire your first handgun. The local police should be in a position to advise, but as firearm legislation is a complex subject it may be necessary to go to a fairly senior level to get reliable answers. Even then, the advice may be wrong. If possible, get a written statement setting out the position so that it is difficult for anyone to claim that they misunderstood your intentions or did not say what you say they said! You should also contact any local or national societies involved with collecting or shooting because such societies are often better informed on the law than the police.

THE REIGN OF TERROR IN IRELAND—A LESSON IN THE ART OF SELF-DEFENCE.

A B O V E

This rather cheap-looking weapon, the Liberator, was intended to play a part in the battles of World War II, to be dropped in quantities to *various resistance groups fighting the Japanese in the Pacific. It is valued by some collectors as an oddity.*

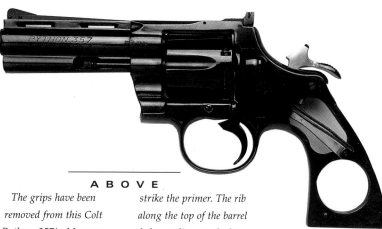

A B O V E

The grips have been removed from this Colt Python .357in Magnum revolver to show the source of the power—the main spring, which forces the hammer down to *strike the primer. The rib along the top of the barrel helps to disperse the heat created by the shots, because the barrel can get very hot.*

R I G H T

This curious looking weapon is a squeeze or palm pistol. It was designed to be held in the clenched fist, with the barrel projecting between the fingers. To fire a shot, the fist was clenched, which squeezed in the curved bar (the trigger) at *the rear. The 8mm weapon, which was primarily intended as a self-defense pistol, was* *named The Protector, and it was patented by a Frenchman, Turbiaux, in 1882.*

CARE OF ACQUISITIONS

Having cleared the first hurdle and found out that it is possible for you to collect the weapons, some preparation is necessary before you make your first acquisition. You must consider how you are going to store your collection, and some of the factors to be considered are security, recording and insurance.

Security Security is important because some police forces will insist on certain standards depending on the location and the likely size and nature of your proposed collection. The intrinsic value of the guns and the importance of preventing criminal use are both factors that make it essential that the guns are safely and securely protected. Safes are an obvious storage point, but, of course, this means that the collection will not be seen on open display. Special cabinets with security glass doors and panels are available, and there are many types of alarm. Trigger locks can ensure that the actions are not worked, and, of course, ammunition and guns should never be kept together unless under strict supervision. Needless to say, all these precautions will cost money and sometimes the charges can be quite high.

Display Display and security are closely connected, and compromise is usually the only solution. If the weapons are kept under glass it is important to ensure that they are not in direct sunlight, for the sun is a marvelous bleaching agent, lightening and drying the wood. Ideally, the weapons should not be handled with bare hands, for human hands, for human sweat is a powerful rusting agent. Even present-day bluing is affected by some sweat, and thin cotton gloves should be worn at all times when handling the weapons. The material on which the guns rest should ideally be chemically inactive and certainly acid free.

Recording Having acquired an item for the collection the first job—after a quiet gloat—is to record the piece. It is well worth creating a fairly full catalogue right from the start of your collection. Quite apart from keeping a personal record, if the unfortunate should happen and an item be stolen, you will be able to provide your insurance company and the police with a full description. The important details to note are the small features that can distinguish one similar item from another. Numbers, marks, scratches, wear, measurements, weight, and replacement parts can all help to identify a particular weapon.

The catalogue description will be greatly enhanced by the addition of a photograph, which ideally should be as detailed as possible—a tiny smudgy print will be of little help. One full-length shot together with one or two close-ups of any particular features will usually suffice. Modern Polaroid and SLR cameras are now so simple and effective that taking such photographs should not be too difficult.

Details of the price and place of purchase and subsequent disposal should all be recorded. In the interests of privacy it is as well to record the price by means of a simple code, substituting letters for figures.

Insurance In these uncertain times insurance is essential and there are companies who will insure collections. They will require a complete list of the items, with full descriptions and a valuation. It may be necessary to obtain an authenticated valuation from a professional, for which a charge will be made. In general, it is customary to fix the insurance about a third higher than actual value, for it is inevitable that the cost of replacing an item will exceed the original price paid.

Inevitably the question of insurance and values raises the question of what to pay for any item. The only realistic answer is as much as you want or can afford. There is never a set fixed price for a collector—even brand-new pistols can be haggled over—and it is impossible to assign a specific price to every individual piece. There are so many variables. Scarcity and condition are two of the most important aspects to consider, but other factors are the amount of restoration, replacement, or renovation that has been carried out and whether there are any special features about a particular weapon that make it especially desirable to the collector. All these and other points will need to be considered. If one of the books that lists values is used for reference, it must be remembered that

ABOVE
Carried by many French staff officers as their official side arm, Le Française 6.35mm pistol illustrated top is Type Policeman, and is unusual in that the movement of the slide does not cock the action. Another slightly unusual feature of Le Française was the forward-breaking movement of the barrel, (bottom).

the figures given will apply only to the particular item described or illustrated. In different circumstances a similar piece could sell at a very different price. All such lists are, and can only be, generalizations.

In the end, the question to be answered is how badly is the piece wanted. If there is a real desire, caution rather goes to the wall and a price in excess of the usual will be paid. To balance the feeling of consternation, it can be argued that if a particular piece was a little expensive at the time, in a year or so it will probably seem very reasonable.

DECORATED STOCKS AND BARRELS

The 16th and 17th centuries saw the personal firearm develop from a crude piece of weaponry into a possession reflecting the wealth and prestige of its owner; barrels were often chiseled in relief and gilt, while stocks were fitted with mounts of gilt and inlaid bronze. Such pieces are among the most sought-after items for serious collectors.

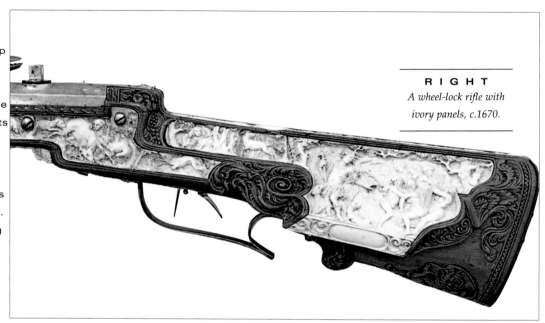

RIGHT
A wheel-lock rifle with ivory panels, c.1670.

BELOW
Two Turkish flintlocks: 18th century (top) and 17th century (below).

RIGHT
Detail of a German wheel-lock pistol, dated 1579.

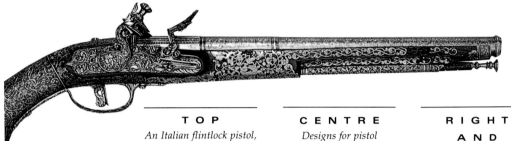

TOP

*An Italian flintlock pistol,
c.1690.*

CENTRE

*Designs for pistol
ornamentation by
Simonin of Paris, 1685.*

**RIGHT
AND
BOTTOM**

*A flintlock pistol by an
unknown French
gunsmith, c.1690.*

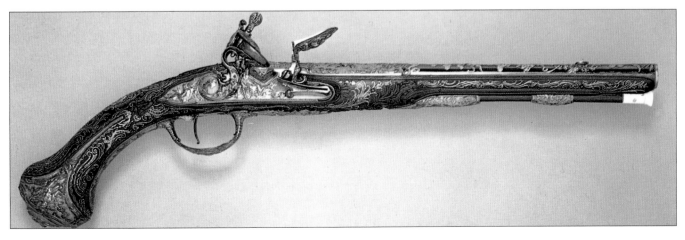

REPLICAS AND RELATED KEEPSAKES

BLACK POWDER is a vintage propellant, an explosive mixture of charcoal, sulfur and potassium nitrate (saltpeter). It was used from the dawn of the firearms era to the end of the 19th century, when it was finally replaced by smokeless powders, mixtures of nitrocellulose and nitroglycerine. Black powder was not suited to automatic weapons because of its inefficient, low-pressure combustion and the thick acid residue it left behind on firing. The use of black powder in service revolvers also diminished for the same reasons, but the propellant was still used in muzzle-loaded firearms as they could not cope with the pressures generated by smokeless powders.

Today, many firearms enthusiasts still enjoy shooting with percussion- and flint-ignited black powder handguns, and the lack of suitable genuine antique weapons has prompted Italian and American manufacturers to produce authentic replicas of early Colt, Remington, and Rodgers & Spencer revolvers. Some also produce kit form versions of early single barreled flintlocks and percussion pistols, so that shooters can immerse themselves totally in their hobby.

International match target shooting takes place with muzzle-loaders, which are surprisingly accurate, and the search for greater accuracy has led to some very fine examples of pistolcraft: the German 1858 Remington replica by Hege is better made and more expensive than many good quality center-fire pistols and revolvers.

The interest in muzzle-loading also prompted Ruger in the United States to make a "modern" black powder revolver based on its blackhawk lockwork. The revolver also has adjustable sights and a cylinder spindle shroud to reduce fouling and jamming of the cylinder during extended shooting sessions.

The bulk of the replica revolvers are made in Italy by Uberti and Armi San Marco. Their sales are worldwide, and are very popular in France, who do not place the same restrictions on ownership of muzzle-loaders as they do on other handguns. Many replicas are made in stainless steel as well as in the traditional, blued carbon steel, as the effects of the acid corrosion on firing is not so marked on stainless steel.

EPHEMERA

Shooting and guns have always proved attractive subjects for writers, and printers have been kept busy supplying a wide range of printed

RIGHT
Replica Le Mat percussion revolver.

BELOW
Pedersoli Le Page replica.

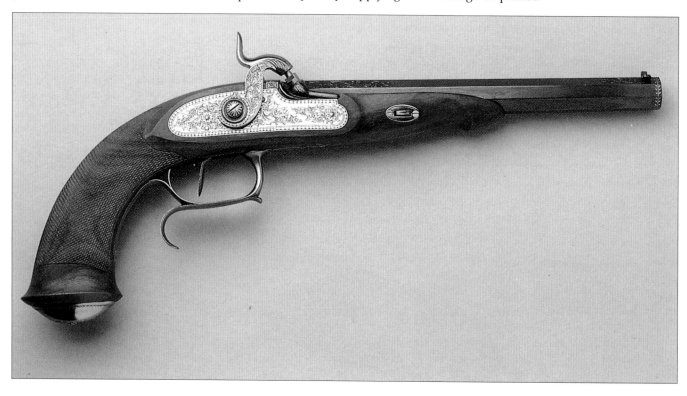

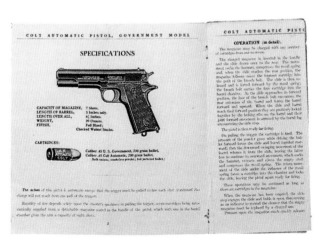

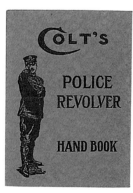

From left to right: A leaflet for the Colt 1911A1, which was supplied with the weapon on purchase; it is undated but must postdate 1921, when the design was

ABOVE

altered. A 24-page promotional booklet for the police, dated 1913; it contains instructions on the use and care of the Colt revolver. A folding booklet for the Colt 1911

automatic pistol; the booklet predates 1921. Early examples of this type of leaflet are fairly rare, and they are seldom seen in such good condition as these.

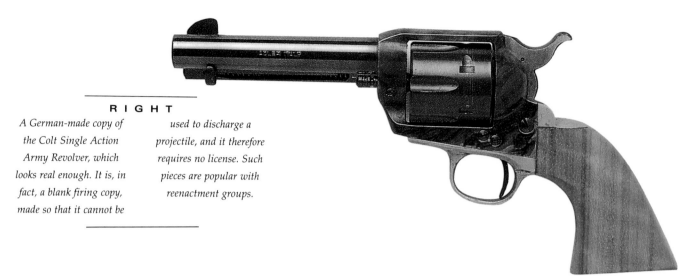

RIGHT

A German-made copy of the Colt Single Action Army Revolver, which looks real enough. It is, in fact, a blank firing copy, made so that it cannot be used to discharge a projectile, and it therefore requires no license. Such pieces are popular with reenactment groups.

material in addition to books. For those with an interest in guns there is a wide range of peripheral—often paper—material, usually known as ephemera, just waiting to be collected.

Much ephemera is very fragile and liable to destruction, but some, such as old catalogues, is a little more durable. During the later part of the 19th century most gunsmiths offered an extremely wide range of items for the shooter, and they issued catalogues that were often well printed. There are mines of information, and those produced by some of the larger firms are almost textbooks of contemporary firearms. Most are well illustrated and often include brief explanations of the products. It is an interesting, if somewhat depressing, pastime to look at prices and compare them with current ones. Obviously it is much more interesting if the genuine article can be found, but modern reprints of the old catalogues should not be disregarded for they contain a wealth of detail.

Gunmakers also advertised fairly widely, and it is always worthwhile scanning contemporary newspapers or magazines for such insertions. Ideally, the page with the advertisement on it should be kept intact, but such are the pressures on living space that it may be necessary to clip them. If this is done it is vital to note the source, including the name of newspaper and, most importantly, the date. Some of the bigger manufacturers and suppliers often rose to special occasions and distributed leaflets to encourage sales or warn of problems, but these are fairly rare as their working life was very short.

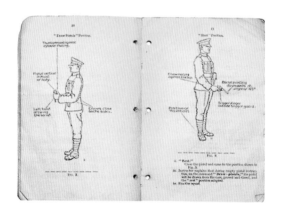

Trade cards are another rare item, for by their nature they were giveaway, throwaway items. Nevertheless, examples still survive and turn up at ephemera fairs. The trade labels that were stuck inside cases are seldom found apart from the cases, but some collectors in the past unwisely removed them and they may very occasionally appear. A number of these labels have been copied and aged and distressed to fool the enthusiast, but a close look at the texture of the print with a small lens will probably enable an accurate decision on authenticity to be made.

Interest in things military and shooting seems to have been much more widespread in the later part of the 19th century and the early years of the 20th century. Many magazines and newspapers carried articles on the latest developments in the arms field, and these are worth seeking out in contemporary publications.

THE SINGLE barreled pistols of the 16th century were the forebears of the modern handgun and many of their qualities of simplicity, reliability and strength are replicated in the single shot cartridge pistols that are being produced today.

Modern, single shot pistols are not used for defense or for military assaults but for sporting purposes: either target shooting or handgun hunting. In Europe, target shooting broadly follows the doctrines of the Union International de Tir, the UIT, which encompasses international rimfire and center-fire target pistol shooting. All of the center-fire disciplines, and all but one of the rimfire ones, require the delivery of multiple shots in a short time, so the single shot pistol is not suitable, due to its slow speed of use.

The Olympic discipline, Free Pistol, has no such constraints, since 60 shots need to be fired at 50 meters in two and a half hours. This has led to the development of highly specialized, single shot pistols with "orthopedic" grips to wrap around the hand, and electronic release triggers for the shortest possible lock time—the time taken for the cartridge to be ignited from when the trigger is squeezed. All free pistols are in .22 LR rimfire caliber. Most European single shot pistols are chambered for .22 LR; exceptions to this are the bolt action Anschutz

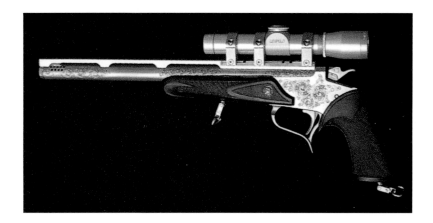

A B O V E
Customized SSK conversion of single shot Thompson/Center Contender.

L E F T
American single shot pistols like the RPM XL are used at long range for hunting or for steel target shooting.

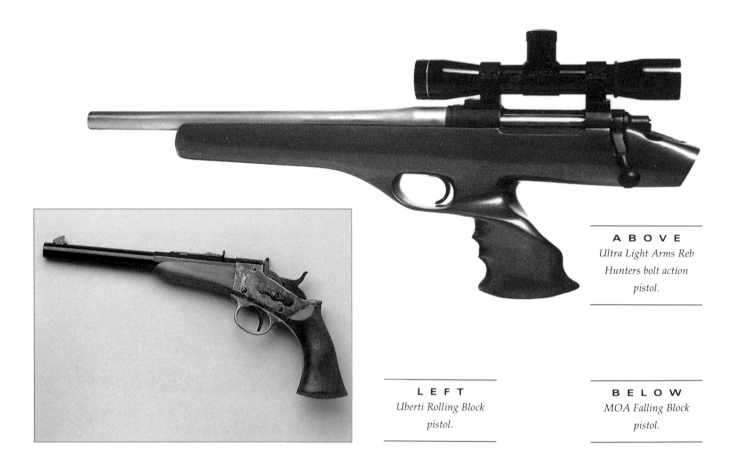

A B O V E

Ultra Light Arms Reb Hunters bolt action pistol.

L E F T

Uberti Rolling Block pistol.

B E L O W

MOA Falling Block pistol.

Drulov .22 target pistol.

*Hämmerli Model 152
Electronic Free Pistol.*

*Morini CM 80 Free
pistol.*

LEFT
*Small caliber European
self-loading pistols have
proved very popular for
precision target shooting.
Top & lower left: .32 and
.22 versions of the
Walther GSP.
Lower right: Hämmerli
208.*

Exemplar, which is also available in .22 WMR, and the hand-built British Kengils, used for long-range pistol shooting and made in calibers up to .308 Win.

In the United States, however, there has been far more scope for large caliber, single shot pistols since the introduction of long-range target shooting at heavy steel plate targets (known as silhouette shooting), and the acceptance of handgun hunting for large and small game. The strength of single shot pistols is very high in relation to their weight, so very powerful cartridges can be chambered, including a number of rifle calibers.

There are many diverse action types available for single shot pistols despite the apparent simplicity of the single chambered barrel. One of the most popular actions is the "break-top," which hinges upward just forward of the breech when unlatched, giving access to the chamber.

This allows a simple hammer and trigger to be used in a common frame, and a range of barrels can be easily interchanged. This versatility is best illustrated by the Thompson/Center Contender pistol which can use the same action for calibers from .22 LR up to .357 Herret and .44 Magnum. The Contender action is used by hunting pistol builder J. D. Jones of SSK Industries, who has developed the SSK Handcannons which fire a range of "wildcat", nonstandard calibers for hunting.

Bolt actions derived from rifles are used on some single shot pistols such as the Remington XP-100 for strength with high-powered rifled cartridges. One lesson that is slow to be learnt by some bolt action pistol makers is that for a right-handed shooter, it is far easier to operate the bolt with the left hand while at the same time maintaining a strong grip on the pistol with the gun hand.

RIGHT
*The M14/M1A is still in
use by target shooters for
their High Power rifle
match.*

WILDCAT PISTOLS AND HANDGUNS

A WILDCAT CARTRIDGE is one that is not made commercially. Many of the popular sporting cartridges on sale today started life as wildcats, being developed from existing components by professional and amateur enthusiasts. At first, wildcats were mainly improved forms of rifle ammunition. When there appeared to be a need for a better ballistic performance from an action length of barrel bore diameter, the experimenters would take standard cases and reduce or expand the neck size, blow the case out and alter shoulder angles to increase propellant capacity, or even cut down the overall length of case reforming and reaming the neck. One of the most famous wildcatters was P. O. Ackley and many of the successful cartridge designs are due to him, the .30–06 Ackley Improved being one of the most popular. If a wildcat becomes very popular, ammunition companies start producing the cartridges for sale and firearms manufacturers chamber their wares for them. The .243 Winchester, a popular deer-hunting cartridge started life as a wildcat, as did the rifle cartridges .280 Remington, .308 Norma Magnum, 6mm Remington, and 8mm Remington Magnum. It is worth noting that the new rifle calibers use existing size barrel bores and bullets; it is only the chamber and the case that holds the propellant that are redesigned.

Wildcats for revolvers and self-loading pistols have also been made, the simpler versions usually necking down a large caliber to a smaller one to gain higher muzzle velocity. Some of the recent really high performance cartridges all started life from cut down rifle cases. .375 Super Mag was derived from .375 Winchester, .475 Linebaugh is made from .45–70 brass, .475 Wildey Magnum originally used cut down and reamed .284 Winchester cases; and .44 AutoMag did the same thing with .308 Winchester.

Bolt action It is no surprise that some of the single shot pistols made today have essentially Mauser type rifle actions to cope with high pressure ammunition. One of the most popular is Remington's bolt action XP100 chambered for 7mm Bench Rest (7mm BR), a shortened and necked-down version of the rifle caliber .308 Winchester. 7mm BR Ammunition is produced

A B O V E

The original Deringer pistols were single shot defence pieces, but the name was corrupted to "derringer" and applied to small multi-barrelled handguns. The COP pistol has four fixed barrels and a rotating striker which fires each .357 Magnum cartridge in turn.

A B O V E

Single shot pistols have lent themselves to "wildcatting", the practice of making new ammunition calibres to satisfy ballistic theories. Illustrated is one of the author's wildcats, .355 AdaMatic (center) which is 10mm Auto (right) necked down to take 9mm bullets from 9mm Luger (left) for use in a self-loading pistol.

by Remington with a 140 grain (9.1 g) pointed soft point bullet that leaves a 15in (381mm) barrel at 2,215 fps (674 mps) with a muzzle energy of 1,525 ft lb (2066 joules). In 1989 Remington introduced 6mm BR ammunition, which used a lighter 100 grain (6.5 g) bullet which reached 2550 fps (777 mps) and an energy of 1,444 ft lb (1957 joules). The 6mm BR has a very flat trajectory, dropping less than six inches (152mm) at 200 yards (183 m). As a comparison, a .44 Magnum handgun firing 240 grain (15.5 g) bullets at 1,500 fps (457 mps) would have a 200 yard bullet drop of over 30in (762mm). Remington's XP100 long range pistol is also made in the rifle calibers .223 Remington (5.6mm), .250 Savage, 7mm–08 Remington, and .35 Remington, in left- and right-handed versions. Rifle makers Ultra Light Arms Inc. of Granville, West Virginia, also makes left- and right-handed bolt action pistols based on its rifle action. For a right-handed person it is more convenient to work the bolt of a rifle with the right hand, stabilizing the firearm with the left arm and right shoulder. A long-range handgun has no shoulder stock, however, and it is easier to keep a grip on the butt with the right hand and work a bolt with the left, otherwise the pistol has to be turned on its side to operate the action, or the grip changed. The Ultra Light Hunter's pistol is made in most calibers from .22–250 to .308 Winchester, and it has the advantage of an integral 5-round magazine. Both the XP100 and the Ultra Light have barrels of 14in (356mm) in length and weigh 4 lb (1.81 kg).

Falling block pistols Falling block actions were popular with riflemakers during the 19th century due to their strength and accuracy. Ruger still produces a falling block rifle and the MOA Corporation of Dayton, Ohio, makes falling block pistols. The basic design is very simple. A fixed barrel and chamber is closed by a solid bolt of steel that rises up behind the cartridge when a lever in front of the trigger is pulled to the rear. To remove a cartridge the lever is pushed forward, the steel bolt is lowered and a spring loaded extractor lifts the case a little way out. (This is known as primary extraction.) A fresh cartridge can then be

inserted by hand and the bolt closed again. A magazine cannot easily be used with falling block actions, and none are available for current production arms.

Like bolt-action pistols, falling block handguns can be chambered for virtually any pistol or rifle caliber within reason. They both have permanently fixed, screwed in barrels, although the MOA pistol can be supplied with additional factory fitted barrels in other calibers. In order to demonstrate the strength of their pistol, the MOA Corporation have made one chambered for .460 Weatherby Magnum, one of the most powerful bolt-action rifle cartridges made. The handgun was fixed in a machine rest, loaded and fired. There was no damage to the pistol, but the machine rest was ripped from the mountings, and the shooting booth lost some decor due to the muzzle blast. The .460

A B O V E
The sport of long range handgun shooting is focused on knocking down steel silhouette targets, which requires a powerful and flat shooting cartridge. As a result, many of the single shot handguns are chambered for rifle cartridges.

ABOVE

The Pachmayr Dominator will also convert a 1911 pistol into a powerful single shot handgun.

LEFT

The Thompson/Center Contender was first sold in 1967 and is the biggest selling break-top pistol in the world, chambered for over 40 standard calibers in its history.

The rugged action of the Contender is used by J. D. Jones of SSK Industries to build his Handcannon hunting pistols. SSK makes new barrels to fit the Contender receiver, and they are chambered for Jones's own wildcat cartridges, which have the suffix JDJ after the caliber. The power of these founds is remarkable and Jones has used them for hunting all types of game. He is one of the few people to have taken all of the "big five" African game with a handgun, a list that includes lion, elephant, and rhinoceros. Three basic cartridges are used for most JDJ wildcats: .225 Winchester (up to 7mm JDJ), .444 Marlin (those larger to .430), and .45–70 (used for .475 JDJ). Both base cases are rimmed to allow easy extraction from the chamber. The most powerful of the JD Jones cartridges, .475 JDJ will reach 1,500 fps (457 mps) with a 500 grain (32.4mm) bullet giving an energy of 2,500 ft lb (3,388 joules), Jones has made some even "wilder" wildcats in his time. One was just .358 Winchester necked up to .375in (9.5mm) and had the name .375 JRS— Jones Rhino Stomper. Another used a shortened and rebated .460 Weatherby case that was belled out to take a .50in (12.7mm) bullet and was made for use in Remington XP action. Jones stopped adding powder when he reached 1,800 fps (549 mps) with a 600 grain bullet because he thought the pistol might shake apart with the shock. The muzzle energy generated, 4,318 ft lb (5,850 joules), gave considerable recoil in the pistol, which weighed just 5 lb (2.3 kg), including the telescopic sight. Illustrated is the SCI commemorative pistol, made in 1986 on a Contender action. The detail shows the engraving on the side of the action and the gold inlay at the muzzle, beneath the recoil reducing ports.

R I G H T
J. D. Jones builds his hunting SSK Handcannons on Contender actions. Illustrated is the SCI commemorative pistol made in 1986.

JD JONES AND SSK HANDGUNS

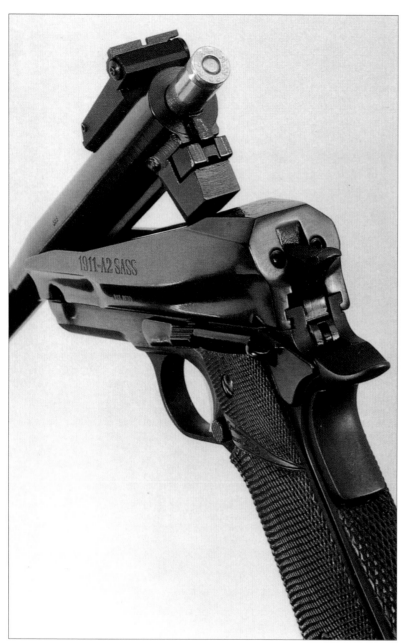

Springfield Armory's 1911–A2 SASS conversion turns a 1911A1 self-loading pistol in to a break-top single shot that can fire rifle cartridges.

which locks shut. To fire, an external hammer must be thumbed back before squeezing the trigger.

One of the main advantages of the break-top pistol is that a single receiver and trigger group can be used with a wide range of barrels. This increases the shooter's caliber options at very low cost. Two US manufacturers, Springfield Armory and Pachmayr, sell conversion kits to change 1911 type self-loading pistols into potent single-shot handguns in a variety of calibers. Springfield's Model 1911–A2 SASS (Springfield Armory Single Shot) has two barrel lengths and eight assorted caliber options, .22 LR, .223 Remington, 7mm Bench Rest, 7mm–08, .308 Winchester, .358 Winchester, and .44 Magnum. The most powerful of these is .358 Winchester. From a rifle's 24in (610mm) barrel .358 Win will drive a 200 grain (13 g) bullet to 2,530 fps (771 mps). This would probably drop to 1,800 fps (549 mps) from the SASS's 14.9in (378mm) barrel if correctly loaded, still giving an impressive 1,440 ft lb (1,951 joules) of muzzle energy. The choice of calibers is similar for the Pachmayr Dominator with the exception of .358 Win.

The other manufacturers of break-top pistols are all in the United States. They offer most of the powerful pistol and revolver calibers, and a number of rifle calibers up to .308 Winchester. They include: Competition Arms, Ithaca, RPM, Thompson/Center, and Wichita.

Thompson/Center Contender The Contender pistol designed in 1967 by Warren Center and manufactured by Thompson/Center Arms is the leading break-top. It was the first modern break-top, and since 1967 has been offered in over 40 chamberings, although the list had reduced to less than half of that by 1990. The caliber options over the six barrel variants are: .22 LR, .22 Win Mag, .22 Hornet, .222 Remington, .223 Remington, .270 REN, 7mm TCU, 7–30 Waters, .30–30 Win, .32–20 Win, .357 Magnum, .357 Rem Maximum, .35 Remington, 10mm Auto, .44 Magnum, .445 Super Mag, .45–70 Government, and .45 Colt. The .445 Super Mag and .45–70 Government are the most powerful cartridges, but the story of the Contender does not end there.

Weatherby is not offered as a standard chambering for the MOA pistol, but there are 20 others to choose from including popular rifle and pistol calibers.

Break-top pistols One of the most popular ways to make a single shot pistol is to use a break-top action, similar to that of a traditional break-top shotgun. The action is kept closed by a cross-bolt and opened with a lever. The barrel tips forward and down, allowing insertion of a cartridge. Lifting the barrel up closes the action

WILDCAT RIFLES AND CARTRIDGES

No story on high-performance magazine rifles would be complete without the tale of Roy Weatherby and the rifles and ammunition he created. Like many keen hunters, Weatherby began wildcatting, and produced ammunition with a higher performance than that available commercially. In 1937 his experiments with cartridge case capacity and bullet speeds convinced him that the velocity of the projectile was more important than bullet weight or diameter in comparing the relative killing powers of different ammunition. Trajectory was flatter too, and the shock of a very high velocity bullet seemed to bowl thin-skinned animals over quite easily. In 1945, Weatherby began marketing his high velocity cartridges, chambering conventional actions for them. In 1958 Weatherby brought out what he considered to be the best high pressure action for his ammunition. Instead of the conventional two lugs at the bolt face to lock in to the receiver, the Mk5 action had nine locking lugs in three groups of three. The end of the bolt is in effect screwed into the receiver as a round is chambered, and the bolt face itself is counter-bored to enclose the head of the cartridge case. There are now 10 Weatherby Magnum calibers, all using belted rimless cases. They are all among the most powerful in their caliber class.

The most popular mid-range Weatherby calibers are chambered by a number of manufacturers other than Weatherby themselves. The full list of Weatherby Magnum calibers is: .224, .240, .257, .270, 7mm; .300, .340, .378, .416, and the most powerful of all production magazine rifle calibers at the time of writing, .460 Weatherby Magnum. The big .460 fires a 500 grain (52.4 g) bullet at 2,700 fps (823 mps) at the muzzle with an energy of 8,092 ft lb (10,965 joules). At 100 yards the striking energy of .460 WM exceeds the muzzle energy of all but .500 Jeffrey. At 200 yards the energy is greater than the muzzle energy of .416 Rigby and .425 Westley Richards. At 300 yards the energy is still greater than .338 Win Mag as it leaves the barrel. At 400 yards the striking energy surpasses the 7.62mm NATO (.308 Win) military service round at the muzzle.

A-SQUARE WILDCATS

No one cartridge can be called the most powerful for any length of time, because wildcatters are always making new calibers of ammunition. The A-Square wildcats of Arthur B. Alphin resulted from the failure of a .458 Winchester cartridge when it was fired at a Cape buffalo in 1974. Alphin set about designing cartridges with more stopping power and based them all on the .460 Weatherby case. Most of the cartridges need the long action and magazine used for Rigby and Weatherby ammunition, except for .460 Short A-Square, which is cut back so that it can be used in the shorter .458 Winchester action.

The highest energies generated by the recommended hand-loads in the A-Square range are:

While the .500 A-Square has a lower velocity and muzzle energy than .460 Weatherby, the TKO Factor for it is higher at 105 compared with 89 for the .460. Many believe that this will give the A-Square cartridge the upper hand in the battle for the title of the most powerful sporting magazine rifle cartridge in the world.

CALIBER	BULLET WT		MUZZLE VELOCITY		MUZZLE ENERGY	
	GRAINS	(GRAMS)	FPS	(MPS)	FT LBS	(JOULES)
.338 A-Square	300	19.4	2915	888	5600	7588
.460 Short A-Square	500	32.4	2435	742	6580	8916
.495 A-Square	600	38.9	2280	695	6925	9384
.500 A-Square	600	38.9	2452	747	8106	10984

ACP Abbreviation for cartridge designation "Automatic Colt Pistol."

Action Generalized description of part or all of a firearm's mechanism concerned with loading and/or firing, eg "bolt action," "Martini action."

AE Abbreviation for cartridge designation "Action Express."

A-Square Brand name of the A-Square Co. in Madison, Indiana, manufacturers of rifles and ammunition.

Auto 1) Suffix to cartridge designation indicating that the round is designed for use in self-loading pistols; 2) Shortened form of "automatic" that is often applied to self-loading pistols. These are generally "semiautomatic" rather than "fully automatic."

Automag Brand name for high-powered self-loading pistols and ammunition originally made during the early 1970s. The name is perpetuated on pistols produced by US firms iAi and AMT.

Back action Trigger mechanism where the lockwork is located behind the breech.

Belling out Part of wildcat cartridge manufacture which increases the diameter of the case mouth to take a larger than standard bullet.

Belted case cartridge Cartridge with an external strengthening ring at the head.

Belted Magnum Description of high-powered rifle ammunition which has an external strengthening ring on the head of the cartridge case.

Black powder Also known as gunpowder. Black powder is a mixture of 75 per cent potassium nitrate (saltpeter), 15 percent charcoal, and 10 percent sulfur. The earliest form of reliable propellant known it is still used in antique and replica "muzzle loading" weapons, but has been superseded by nitrocellulose and nitroglycerine based propellants for modern handguns.

Blowback Operating method of small caliber self-loading pistols. The breech block is held closed by spring pressure which, with the inertia of the breech block, holds the cartridge in the chamber of the barrel on firing. Once inertia is overcome by recoil, the breech moves back freely controlled by the recoil spring, ejecting the fired case and loading a fresh cartridge into the chamber.

Bluing Otherwise known as "blacking." Controlled corrosion of the surface of ferrous steel that results in a thin inert blue/black layer on the surface, offering some protection against further corrosion.

Bolster Thickened and rounded area of a double rifle's action used to increase strength.

Bolt action Description of a firearm loading mechanism which uses a manually operated bolt to lock the cartridge in the chamber.

Bottlenecked Description of a cartridge which steps down to a smaller diameter from the base of the case to the neck. Usually seen in rifle ammunition, but also used in a few self-loading pistol calibers.

Boxlock Trigger mechanism where the locks are contained in a closed box below the breech.

Break-top Handgun, shotgun, or rifle which is loaded or unloaded by unlatching the barrel and chamber/cylinder and swinging it down to open the breech. Typical examples are the Webley revolvers, Thompson/Center Contender pistols and double-barreled rifles.

Breech (breach) The end of a barrel in which combustion takes place when the weapon is fired.

Breech-loading Description of firearm used with cartridges that are inserted into an open breech to load. The breech is closed with a bolt, slide, falling block, or lever to contain pressure during firing.

Broomhandle Nickname given to the Mauser Model C1896 pistol which had a distinctive wooden butt.

Brush cartridge General description of a moderate to high-powered cartridge which is used for short range hunting.

Bullet Shaped projectile fired from a firearm. Generally made from a lead alloy and often covered with a copper or steel coating for use in high velocity ammunition. "Bullet" does not refer to a complete round of ammunition.

Bullpup Shortened rifle action which places the magazine behind the trigger rather than in front of it. Though it shortens the overall length of the firearm, it limits the use of firing from only one shoulder.

Burst fire Trigger mechanism that permits firing of more than one round of ammunition with each pull of the trigger. Interrupters stop each burst after a preset number of rounds (usually two or three). Burst fire should not be confused with fully automatic fire, which will only stop

when the trigger is released or the magazine emptied.

Caliber (calibre) 1) Measurement of the bore of a firearm mode across the lands of the rifling. It is the bore of the barrel after subtracting the depth of the rifling grooves. 2) Name given to cartridge designation of a weapon and ammunition which may or may not be the same as the exact bore of the firearm.

Cam Projection or lug on a barrel or bolt which changes the direction of the component under linear force.

Cartridge Complete round of ammunition comprising case, primer, propellant, and bullet.

Center-fire Cartridges that have a central primer or percussion cap in the need of the cartridge case.

Chamber Part of the barrel or cylinder that contains the cartridge on firing.

Cylinder Major component of a revolver containing chambers that hold the cartridges and brings them in line with the barrel as the hammer/trigger is cocked.

Dagg Name given to early wheel-lock pistols.

Delayed blowback Mechanism for preventing the breech block opening in a self-loading weapon until the bullet has left the barrel and the breech pressure has dropped. Most common is the Browning delayed blowback system which keeps the barrel locked into the side with lugs until the pressure drops, whereupon the barrel cams down and permits the slide to cycle by blowback. The Walther/Beretta wedge delayed blowback system also locks the slide and barrel using a pivoting wedge which is forced down by an internal rod as the slide moves backward.

Derringer Originally a large bore single-shot pistol sold by Philadelphia gunsmith Henry Deringer. The name has been corrupted to derringer and is most commonly used to describe small 2-shot handguns.

Disconnector Internal device in a self-loading weapon that prevents fully automatic fire and necessitates the release of the trigger before firing subsequent shots.

Double action (DA) Description of trigger mechanism that can be cocked and fired by pulling the trigger or can be manually cocked by pulling back the hammer which results in a lighter trigger pull. Also applied to the trigger-cocking shooting method.

Express 1) Shortened form of "Express Train," a description used for a high velocity Purdey rifle mode in 1856. Adapted at the end of the century for high velocity ammunition with a flat trajectory. 2) Description of open sights fitted to big game rifles that are swift to align with the target.

Exterior ballistics Study of the flight of a projectile through the air after it has left a firearm's barrel.

Falling block Type of breech-loading action using a block of steel which rises vertically to close the chamber.

FBI Federal Bureau of Investigation, an arm of the US Department of Justice.

FFg Measurement of grain size of black powder propellant. FFg is large and slow burning, FFFFg is small and fast burning.

Firepower Term given to combination of cyclic rate or ammunition capacity of a firearm along with the power of individual cartridges.

Flintlock 17th-century firearm ignition system in which a flint clamped in a swinging arm was propelled by spring pressure against a steel. This resulted in a shower of sparks, which ignited fine black powder placed in a "pan," which in turn ignited the main propellant charge.

Flobert Early rimfire type cartridge design where priming compound covered the entire inside of the cartridge.

FPS Abbreviation for Feet Per Second, an imperial measurement of velocity.

Fulminate Chemical compound which detonates on impact. Mercury Fulminate was used for primers and percussion caps in early firearms. Lead styphnate is used for modern noncorrosive primers.

Gas cutting Erosion of a firearm by the flame and pressure generated during firing.

Gas operation Method of cycling a self-loading firearm using the propellant gases to push back the breech.

Handcannon 1) Brand name for Thompson/Center Contender pistols which have been converted by SSK Industries to fire exceedingly high-powered ammunition for hunting or silhouette shooting; 2) Early hand-held firearm of large bore.

Handload Home manufacture of ammunition by a shooter. Handloading is used to tailor the ammunition to the characteristics of the firearm and the use to which it is put. Handloading can increase accuracy and alter the power of the weapon.

Headspace 1) Distance between the base of the cartridge and the face of the breech; 2) Reference point at which the cartridge is located in the chamber. For revolvers this is usually the rim at the base of the cartridge; for self-loading pistols this is often the mouth of the case at the front of the chamber. Bolt action rifles, with bottlenecked rimless ammunition, headspace on the case shoulder.

H&H Abbreviation of Holland & Holland, a British gun-making company.

Hollowpoint Bullet design with a hollow nose which is designed to expand and mushroom on impact giving greater shock effect. Sometimes erroneously referred to as "Dum Dums."

ISPC International Practical Shooting Confederation. The international controlling body for one type of action or combat-style target shooting.

Kengil Brand name for a British single-shot pistol used for long-range target shooting.

Lands Raised area of rifling that bites into the bullet and imparts stabilizing spin.

Lever action Breech-loading mechanism using a lever to open the breech, eject the fired cartridge case and insert a fresh round of ammunition.

Lock General term for firearm subassembly, which is involved with holding breech closed and/or effecting firing of the cartridge.

Lugs Raised areas on barrels or bolts which engage in mating recesses in the slide or breech.

Machine pistol Small, fully automatic firearm that fires a pistol cartridge. Also known as submachine guns (SMG), but SMG is also applied to some small fully automatic firearms that fire moderate and full power rifle cartridges.

Magnum Originally a cartridge suffix used to denote powerful high-pressure ammunition or high velocity. Now appears on some new low-pressure calibers as a marketing ploy rather than an indication of terminal effectiveness. The

original pistol Magnums, .357 and .44, have been overtaken in the power league by the Maximums, Supermags, and Casull calibers.

Mars High-powered pistol designed by Hugh W. Gabbet-Fairfax at the turn of the 20th century.

Minor caliber Low-scoring band designated by the IPSC for shooters using ammunition where the product of the bullet weight in grains and velocity in feet per second, divided by 1000 is equal to/greater than 125. Originally derived

from the momentum of .38 Special revolver ammunition, it is now based on the momentum of a 115 grain 9mm Luger bullet when fired from a 4in barreled pistol.

MPS Abbreviation of meters per second, a metric measurement of velocity.

Multi caliber Brand name for a conversion to the Colt 1911 pistol by Peters-Stahl in West Germany, which permits different caliber barrels and ammunition to be used with the same frame and slide.

Muzzle End of the barrel from which the projectile emerges during firing.

Muzzle energy Energy of a bullet when it leaves a firearm barrel. Calculated in foot-pounds (ft lbs) from the square of the velocity, multiplied by the bullet weight in pounds, divided by twice the acceleration due to gravity. Since the acceleration due to gravity is a constant, the equation can be reduced to ME=(VxBW)/450240. Also measured in joules, which is the muzzle energy in ft lbs multiplied by 1.355, or in kilogram meters, which is the energy in ft lbs multiplied by 0.1383.

Muzzle loading Method of loading weapons with chambers or barrels closed at one end. Propellant is poured down into the chamber and the bullet or ball projectile rammed down on top. Ignition can be by flint, match, wheel, or percussion cap. Muzzle loaders use low pressure black powder or its substitutes rather than modern high pressure products as propellants.

Muzzle velocity Speed of bullet when it leaves a firearm's barrel. Measured in feet per second (fps) or metres per second (mps).

NATO North Atlantic Treaty Organisation. A military grouping of some Western countries.

Neck down Part of the wildcat cartridge manufacture which decreases the diameter of the case mouth to take a smaller than standard bullet.

Nipple Hollow stub at the breech end of a muzzle loading firearm on to which a percussion cap is placed. When the hammer falls on the percussion cap it is crushed between the hammer and the nipple, exploding and sending a flame through the nipple to the main powder charge.

Nitrocellulose Base material for modern high pressure noncorrosive propellant. Nitrocellulose is mixed with retardants and sometimes nitroglycerine to modify its burning rate and give greater versatility in different weapons.

Peacemaker Alternative name for Colt's Single Action Army model revolver first made in 1872.

Pepperbox Early 19th-century repeating handguns. In effect they were revolvers without a barrel, each chamber being elongated to form a short integral barrel without rifling. Rendered obsolete by the introduction of Colt's revolver, they were still popular until the Civil War.

Percussion Name given to the explosive effect of certain salts or detonating compounds when struck. When the salts are contained in a thin copper cup the result is a percussion cap that is placed on a nipple of a black-powder firearm. Modern primers are also a type of percussion cap which form an integral part of a cartridge.

Power factor Name given to the result of the IPSC Major and Minor caliber calculation.

Power floor Minimum power level for IPSC major and minor power ratings.

Primer Impact sensitive percussion cap used in center-fire ammunition, which is inserted into the center of the cartridge base. Ignites the main propellant charge when struck.

Propellant Principal consumable component of ammunition. When ignited, propellants burn at a very high rate generating high pressure gas. The gas propels the bullet out of the cartridge case and up the barrel of the firearm.

Pyrite Yellow mineral formed from sulfur and iron that was used to create sparks in wheel-lock ignition.

Reaming Rotary removal of metal to enlarge a hole. Used in wildcat cartridge manufacture to thin down the wall of cartridge cases that have been cut back.

Reciprocate Linear movement back and forth. The slide of a pistol reciprocates during firing, as does the breech-block of a self-loading rifle.

Regulation Adjusting a firearm so that the fall of shot is at the same point at the sights. Often used to describe the adjustment of double-barreled rifles so that both barrels shoot to the same point of impact.

Revolver Handgun type which has a fixed barrel and a revolving cylinder.

Rifling Helical grooves inside a firearm barrel that impart stabilizing spin to a bullet as it travels down the bore.

Rimfire Cartridge type in which the priming compound is located in the thin rim of the cartridge case base. One of the first metallic cartridge types, still popular today for target shooting and pest control.

Roller locked Method of creating delayed blowback in self-loading weapons by locking the breech with rollers until the chamber pressure drops.

Round Single unit of ammunition also called a cartridge.

SAA Abbreviation for Colt's Single Action Army model revolver first made in 1872.

Saltpeter (saltpetre) Common name for chemical compound potassium nitrate (KNO_3), a component of black powder (gunpowder).

Sear Component of trigger mechanism that holds hammer or striker back prior to firing.

Self-loading Description of an action type which, when fired, automatically ejects the spent case, recocks the hammer or striker, and chambers a fresh cartridge.

Sidelock Firing mechanism where the lock is mounted on plate fitted to the side of the stock.

Single action (SA) Also known as hammer cocking or thumb cocking in revolvers, where it is necessary to thumb back the hammer in order to index the cylinder and prepare the revolver for firing. Applied to self-loading pistols that cannot be fired by trigger-cocking.

Slide Part of a firearm, usually of a self-loading pistol, which contains the breech block and moves backward and forward during firing and chambering a fresh cartridge.

Smallbore General description of firearms that chamber .22in rimfire ammunition.

Smokeless powder Propellant type based on nitrocellulose, which as introduced at the turn of the 20th century. Produces much less smoke and residue than black powder.

Snaphaunce Early type of flintlock.

Supermag Wildcat cartridge family designed by Elgin Gates of the International Metallic Silhouette Shooting Association (IMSSA).

TKO Taylor Knock Out, a power indicator used by the African hunter, John Taylor. The TKO is calculated by multiplying the bullet diameter in inches by its weight in grains and by the muzzle velocity in feet per second. This figure is then divided by 7000 to arrive at the final TKO force.

Toggle lock Barrel locking system used in Maxim machine-guns, which was adapted by Barchardt and Luger for their self-loading pistols.

Torque Description of the twisting force. Causes rotation under recoil of a firearm.

Trigger-cocking Method of firing a handgun where pulling the trigger cocks then fires the piece. Incorrectly known as "double action," as many handguns have been made that can only fire when trigger-cocked and hence are a form of single action.

Trigger travel Movement of trigger needed before weapon is fired.

UZI Brand name for Israel Military Industries self-loading pistols and machine-guns, from the original designer's name.

Wheel-lock First reliable firearm ignition system dating from the 16th century, in which a steel wheel is spun against iron pyrites to create sparks for propellant ignition.

Wildcat A cartridge that is not made commercially. Wildcats are produced by altering the shape, size, capacity, or caliber of standard cartridge cases.

Win Mag Abbreviation for Winchester Magnum used after caliber to describe a cartridge, e.g. .338 Win Mag.

INDEX

ACKNOWLEDGMENTS

Quintet would like to thank the following for permission to reproduce copyright material. We apologise for any omissions that may have occurred.

ETarchive, Bridgeman Art Library, Mansell Collection, Salamander Books Ltd., Peter Newark's Western Americana, Octopus Books Picture Library, Military Archive and Research Services, Christies, Frank C. Barnes, Birmingham Proof House, Browning Sports Ltd, Coach Harness (UK Uberti and Pedersoli agents), Conjay (UK IMI agents), Edgar Brothers (UK BRNO and Start agents), Framar Shooting World (UK Hämmerli agents), Oliver Gower (UK FAS agent), Gun Digest (USA), Guns Review (UK), Guns and Weapons Magazine, John Harness (Hilton Gun Co), Ian V. Hogg, Walter J. Howe (Shooting Industry Reports), Modern and Antique Firearms (Kengil), Mountain and Sowden, Pro Gun Services, Shooting Developments (Morini agents), John Smart, Jan Stevenson

(Handgunner), Target Gun, Victory Arms, Alan Arnsby, Linda, Andrew and Tony Baldwin, Bob and Barbara Barber, Martin Barber, Tony and Yve Cattermole, Gary Clark, Peter Foulkes, Malcolm Hinds, Arthur Hull, Leyton James, Phil James, Nigel Jennings, John Kenner, Sandy McNab, Bill Martin, John Parry, Steve Parsons, Rodger Saunders, Frank Sitton, Rob Adams, Norma, Sturm, Ruger & Co., Rigby, Weatherby, Steyr Mannlicher, S. Boulter, A. Cutler-Andrews, J. Fielden, N. Green, N. Jennings, W. Martin, Ranger Firearms, Westley Richards and Wildey Inc, Ambrosiana, Milan, Austrian National Library, Vienna, Bayerisches National Museum, Munich, Bradford City Museum, British Museum, Manson & Woods Ltd., London, National Army Museum, London, National Historical Museum, Stockholm, Palazzo Ducale, Venice; Radio Times Hulton Picture Library, Service d'Information et de Relations Publiques des Armées, Sotheby's, London, Tøjhusmeet, Copenhagen, Tower of London (Crown Copyright, Department of the Environment, London), University of Gottingen, Victoria and Albert Museum, London, Helen Downton.